FLYING WITH THE EAGLE,

RACING THE GREAT BEAR

Flying with the Eagle, Racing the Great Bear

Stories From Native North America

Told by Joseph Bruchac

BridgeWater Books

For all of our sons—J. B.

Library of Congress Cataloging-in-Publication Data

Bruchac, Joseph, (date)
  Flying with the eagle, racing the great bear: stories from Native
North America / told by Joseph Bruchac.
    p.   cm.
  Includes bibliographical references.
  Summary: A collection of traditional tales which present the
heritage of various Indian nations, including the Wampanoag,
Cherokee, Osage, Lakota, and Tlingit.
  ISBN 0-8167-3026-1 (lib. bdg.)   ISBN 0-8167-3027-X (pbk.)
  1. Indians of North America—Legends.   2. Indians of North
America—Rites and ceremonies—Juvenile literature.   [1. Indians of
North America—Legends.]   I. Title.
E98.F6B893   1993
[398.2'08997]—dc20   93-21966

Text copyright © 1993 by Joseph Bruchac
Illustrations copyright © 1993 by Murv Jacob

Published by BridgeWater Books, an imprint
of Troll Associates.
Printed in the United States of America.
10 9 8 7 6 5 4 3 2

CONTENTS

FLYING WITH THE EAGLE,

RACING THE GREAT BEAR

INTRODUCTION

There comes a time in every boy's life when he must step into manhood, a time when a boy must leave his home, leave the protection of his mother and father, and go out to prove to himself that he can survive and grow. That fact seems to have been recognized by every human culture. Clearly defined rituals, or rites of passage, were developed to help the young man make that change and better understand the responsibilities of his new adult roles.

Among the more than four hundred different tribal nations that existed in North America before the coming of the Europeans, there were many different rites of passage for young men. The many varieties of the sweat lodge, the practices of fasting in isolation and praying for a guiding vision, and the deeply symbolic ceremonies in which the older men took on the guise of ancestral beings and powerful spirits are among the better-known rites of passage practiced by many Native nations.

One powerful way in which the meanings of this transition have been taught for thousands of years is through traditional stories. Two decades ago, when I first began telling the traditional stories that were part of my own Native heritage, it was to share them with my own children. They were small boys then, but as they grew and changed, my understanding of how the stories worked grew with them.

Many of the stories I've been given are tales designed not only to help the boy find his way to full manhood but also to help the man remember the boy within himself, so that he can be sympathetic and helpful to the coming generations. The old tales grow with us. Now my sons, Jim and Jesse, are young men, telling the stories they learned to the children they teach. That is how the circle of stories works, linking the generations.

Like all the Native American stories I know, the ones in this book are designed both to entertain and to educate. I offer them as a few examples of the ways in which the many different tribal nations of North America recognized the need to guide and gently channel young men as they grew.

I have divided the book into four sections because four is a number of powerful and magical importance to Native peoples: There are four seasons, four winds, four directions, four stages in a person's life. It is interesting in these tales how often each young man faces trials in clusters of four.

One of the reasons I have devoted so much of my own life to the understanding and the respectful telling of traditional Native stories is my strong belief that now, more than ever, these tales have much to teach us— whether we are of Native ancestry or not. We learn about ourselves by understanding others. Our own traditions can be made stronger only when we pay attention to and respect the traditions of people who are different from ourselves. Hearing or reading the stories of the Native peoples of North America will not make any of us Native Americans, but it may help make all of us more human.

THE NORTHEAST

One of the most common rites of passage found throughout most of Native North America is the vision quest. It is known among the Lakota of the western plains as hanblecheyapi, which translates into English as "crying for a vision."

This practice, however, is not limited to the Native American people of the West. As we see in the Anishinabe story "The Dream Fast," it is also present among the peoples of the northeastern woodlands. Many Native people still believe that special guidance is available from the forces of nature and that by fasting and praying in an isolated place, the spiritual senses are sharpened. Animals may come and offer themselves as guides, and a boy may, indeed, find himself flying with the eagle—as we see later on in the book.

The experience a boy has on his first vision quest often shapes the rest of his life. There are many different ways of seeking a vision, but most of them involve going to a place removed from other human beings and

remaining there without food for as long as several days.

The ordeal is also a part of the experience. Going out without the protection of parents, symbolically orphaned as in the story of "White Weasel," is a common theme in these tales. When a boy does this, he may encounter dangerous, even malevolent, forces. The stories tell us he may overcome adversity by making use of the good teachings given him by his elders.

Such recurring themes mirror or sharpen the experiences expected in "real life." Sooner or later, each of us must be like Swift Runner in the Iroquois story "Racing the Great Bear" and challenge our own monsters, with our survival in the balance. These stories tell us that if we have listened well to our elders, we can rely upon ourselves when the need arises.

Finally, "Granny Squannit and the Bad Young Man" remains one of my favorite tales in this section. It is not only a rite-of-passage story but also a good example of the way Native children are disciplined. Beating children or even shouting loudly at them is avoided by Native American parents. Instead, telling lesson stories and speaking calmly and clearly to children to try to lead them in the right direction are common practices. As a last resort, a parent might threaten an unruly child with monsters that prey only upon disobedient children.

Native youngsters are encouraged to refer to elders, whether they are human, animal, or a force of nature, as "Grandmother" or "Grandfather." As a combination of elder and fearful being, Granny Squannit is called upon to help teach a particularly bad boy the proper way to behave.

The Dream Fast
Anishinabe

Long ago, as it still is today, it was the custom for a boy who reached a certain age to go into the forest and wait for a dream. He would build a small lodge and go without food for many days, in the hope he would be visited by some animal or spirit of the forest that would take pity on him and give guidance and power.

There was a boy named Opichi who reached that age. Opichi's father was very respected in the village, and he was determined that his son would be given a dream of such power that no one else could compare with him. So eager was the father for his son to get power that he insisted the boy go on his dream fast before the last snow left the ground, even though most boys would wait until the time when the ground was warm and the leaves returned to the trees.

"My son is strong," said the father. "He will go now. He will gain greater strength from the cold."

Opichi was a boy who always wished to please his parents, and so he did as his father said. They went together into the forest, and the father selected a spot on top of a small hill. There Opichi made a small lean-to of saplings, covering it with hemlock boughs. He sat beneath it on the bare ground with a thin piece of deerskin wrapped about his shoulders.

"I will return each day at dawn," the father said. "You will tell me then what you have seen."

That night the north wind, the icy breath of the Great Bear, blew cold. Opichi's mother was concerned, but the father did not worry. "My son is strong," he said. "This cold wind will make his vision a better one."

3

When the morning came, he went to the lean-to and shook the poles.

"My son," he said, "tell me what you have seen."

Opichi crawled out and looked up at his father. "Father," the boy said, "a deer came to the lodge and spoke to me."

"That is good," said his father. "But you must continue to fast. Surely a greater vision will come to you."

"I will continue to watch and wait," Opichi said.

Opichi's father left his son and went back to his lodge. That night a light snow fell. "I am worried about our son," said Opichi's mother.

"Do not worry," said the father. "The snow will only make whatever dream comes to him more powerful."

When morning came, the father went into the forest again, climbed the hill, and shook the poles, calling his son out.

"Father," Opichi said as he emerged, shaking from the cold, "last night a beaver came to me. It taught me a song."

"That is good," said the father. "You are doing well. You will gain ever more power if you stay longer."

"I will watch and wait," said the boy.

So it went for four more days. Each morning his father asked Opichi what he had seen. Each time the boy told of his experiences from the night before. Now hawk and wolf, bear and eagle had visited the boy. Each day Opichi looked thinner and weaker, but he agreed to stay and wait for an ever-greater vision to please his father.

At last, on the morning of the seventh day, Opichi's mother spoke to her husband. "Our son has waited long enough in the forest. I will go with you this morning, and we will bring him home."

Opichi's mother and father went together into the forest. The gentle breath of the Fawn, the warm south wind of spring, had blown during the night, and all the snow had melted away. As they climbed the hill, they heard a birdsong coming from above them. It was a song they had never heard before. It sounded almost like the name of their son.

> Opi chi chi
> Opi chi chi

When they reached the lodge, Opichi's father shook the poles. "My son," he said, "it is time to end your fast. It is time to come home."

There was no answer. Opichi's mother and father bent down to look into the small lean-to of hemlock boughs and saplings. As they did so, a bird came flying out. It was gray and black with a red chest.

> Opi chi chi
> Opi chi chi

So it sang as it perched on a branch above them. Then it spoke.

"My parents," said the bird, "you see me as I am now. The one who was your son is gone. You sent him out too early and asked him to wait for power too long. Now I will return each spring when the gentle breath of the Fawn comes to our land. My song will let people know it is the time for a boy to go on his dream fast. But your words must help to remind his parents not to make their son stay out too long."

Then, singing that song which was the name of their son, the robin flew off into the forest.

White Weasel
Abenaki

One day, as a hunter was walking through the forest, he heard the sound of a dog howling.

"Someone is in trouble," said the hunter, whose name was Wolverine. He followed the pitiful howling to an abandoned village and found the dog sitting in front of a small wigwam. As soon as it saw Wolverine, it wagged its tail and came over. Then the dog led the hunter inside the wigwam, where a little baby was tied to a cradleboard. The baby was thin and hungry, and his face was covered with scabs.

"Little one," Wolverine said, picking up the child, "I will take pity on you." Then, followed by the dog, he went back to his lodge and handed the baby to his wife, Fisher.

"I give you a child," Wolverine said. "He is starved and sick. He was abandoned to die."

"I am glad to have him," Fisher said. "I will cure him and he will grow strong. Tomorrow I will go out and name him after the first animal I see."

In the morning, Fisher went out into the forest. She had not walked far when a small animal came out of the bushes. It was a little weasel, the color of the newly fallen snow. It was quick in its movements and looked up at her without fear. "You have given my grandson his name," said Fisher. So the boy was named White Weasel.

Wolverine and Fisher cared well for their adopted grandson. They taught him all they knew of hunting and medicine and told him how he was found abandoned.

Many seasons passed, and White Weasel became wiry and strong. He was a good hunter and knew how to use the healing plants of the forest. Finally the day came when he knew he had to leave his foster grandparents.

"Grandfather," he asked Wolverine, "are there other people in the world?"

"Yes," said Wolverine, "but they are far away to the north near the great water."

"I will go there," said White Weasel. "I must find my parents."

"Listen well," Fisher said. "Your parents left you to die. Only your dog, Bad Dog, stayed to watch over you and save your life. You will not know your parents, but your dog will know them. Follow him and he will guide you to them."

"Grandmother," White Weasel said, "I will do as you say. Now I need snowshoes, for I must go to the north."

So Grandmother Fisher made snowshoes from rawhide and ash wood, and White Weasel set out, following his dog.

The boy and his dog traveled north for many days. Then one morning as they were starting out, White Weasel heard the sound of weeping. He looked down to the left of the trail and saw a small man who sat crying. He was one of the little people, the Mikumwesuk.

"Uncle," said White Weasel, "what is wrong?"

"My wife is sick," the little man said. "I know that she will die."

"My grandmother taught me medicine," said White Weasel. "I will help your wife."

Mikumwesu led him through the forest along a twisting path until they came to what looked like a pile of brush. As soon as they went inside, White Weasel saw it was a beautiful lodge. On a pile of rabbit skins was a little woman with a thin, pale face.

"I can cure your sickness," White Weasel said. He gathered herbs and made them into a tea. Mikumwesu's wife drank the tea, and by the morning she was well and strong.

"*Ktsi nidoba*, great friend," said Mikumwesu, "you saved my wife. I will go help you find what you seek." Then White Weasel and Mikumwesu set out together, following the dog. But when the sun was two hands high at midmorning, Mikumwesu stopped near a clearing.

"I must gather spruce gum," he said. He pulled gum from the trees around them, rolled it between his hands, and made six plugs. "Now," Mikumwesu said, "we must put these plugs into our ears. Soon we will need them."

The boy put the plugs into his ears and the ears of his dog. Then he followed Mikumwesu up a cliff. When they looked back toward the path they had left, they saw the trees shaking. Two huge Kiwakwes, the fierce giants of the North, came into the clearing, one from the east and one from the west. As White Weasel watched, the giant from the east threw a stone larger than a wigwam. It shattered when it struck the other giant's chest. Then the giant from the west pulled up a tall pine tree and swung it like a club. It splintered like a twig over the first giant's head. Their mouths were open as they fought, but White Weasel could hear nothing.

The Kiwakwes fought back and forth till the sun was in the middle of the sky. Finally the giant from the east threw the other to the ground and killed him. As White

Weasel and Mikumwesu watched, the Kiwakwe drank the blood of his defeated enemy, then went back into the woods to the east.

Mikumwesu waited a long time before he took the plugs of spruce gum from his ears. White Weasel did the same.

"Look around in the forest below," the little man said.

White Weasel looked. At first he saw nothing. Then he saw many animals—deer, bears, and others—lying dead.

"They were killed by the howling of the giants as they fought," Mikumwesu said. "If we had heard their terrible howls, we also would have died."

Once more they started north, following the little dog. After traveling for four days, Mikumwesu stopped them again.

"We are near the great water," Mikumwesu said. "Tomorrow you must send your small dog ahead to clear the path."

When the morning came, White Weasel said to his dog, "Bad Dog, danger is ahead of us. Go and clear our path so we can travel safely."

Wagging his tail, Bad Dog set out. He had not gone far when he came to two hemlock trees on either side of the trail. Beneath each tree, a huge snake was hidden. Bad Dog breathed in one, two, three, four times. With each breath, he became bigger. When he was taller than the trees, he grabbed one snake and then the other and shook them till they were dead. Then he breathed out one, two, three, four times and was small again.

Wagging his tail, Bad Dog set forth once more. Soon he came to two large stones, one on each side of the

trail. Behind each stone, a great bear was hiding. Again
Bad Dog breathed in four times and grew larger with
each breath. With a growl, he leaped on the bears and
killed each one with a single bite. Then, just as before,
he breathed out four times and was small again.

When White Weasel's dog returned to him, the sun
was four hands high.

"Bad Dog has done well," said Mikumwesu. "Now
the trail is clear. Tomorrow you will reach the village of
the people who killed your parents. All of the people in
that village are bad. They have killed all the other people here in the North. They killed your parents and
pretended to be your father and mother, but your dog
would not let them enter your wigwam. So they left you
there to die."

White Weasel and his dog went along the trail. They
passed between two tall hemlock trees, and White Weasel saw many crows and jays eating something dead.
They passed between two great stones, and White Weasel saw many ravens and foxes eating something dead.
At last they came to a hill. Below them were the great
water and a village on the shore. White Weasel followed
his dog to the first wigwam in the village, where the dog
stopped and growled.

"Wife," said a harsh voice from within, "hear me. Bad
Dog has come."

White Weasel went to the door of the lodge. "*Kwe,*"
he called. "Hello."

"*Kwe,*" the harsh voice called back from within.
"Come inside."

White Weasel and his dog entered the lodge. A man
and woman in beautiful clothing sat by the fire. They
were very attractive, but the boy did not trust what he
saw in their eyes.

"You have found our dog," said the woman. "Give him to us."

"Bad Dog is mine," said White Weasel. "He has protected me since I was a small, sick baby."

The two people looked long and hard at White Weasel. "You are our son," said the man. "Bad Dog carried you off into the forest a long time ago. We are glad to see you. Come and meet the people of our village."

The man who pretended to be White Weasel's father led them out of the lodge. There, by the door, stood Mikumwesu.

"Who is this ugly little man?" said the woman who pretended to be White Weasel's mother.

"You should not insult me," said Mikumwesu. "Soon your village will be covered with sumac trees." The sumacs were the first trees to grow in a deserted village, and Mikumwesu's words were a warning to these people that they would be destroyed.

Many other people began to come out of their lodges. They made fun of White Weasel and Mikumwesu, but the boy and the little man ignored their words.

"My dear son," said the man, "we are glad you have returned. Now we want to play with you. Do you like to wrestle?"

"Yes," said White Weasel, "I am a good wrestler."

"Great friend," said Mikumwesu, reaching into his pouch and drawing the boy aside, "put on these white moccasins. Then you will always land on your feet."

White Weasel put on the moccasins and followed the one who pretended to be his father till they arrived at a big wigwam on a stone ledge near the water. A huge man came out of that wigwam.

"You will wrestle with me," said the big man.

"Grab hold and try to throw me," said White Weasel.

The big man grabbed the boy, lifted him high, and threw him down to break his bones on the rocks. But White Weasel landed lightly on his feet.

"This is fun," said the boy. "Throw me again."

The big man became very angry and threw White Weasel a second time, trying to break his head. Just as before, the boy landed on his feet. Four times the big man tried to kill White Weasel, and four times he failed. Then White Weasel held up his hands.

"Now it is my turn," he said. He lifted the big man up and threw him down so hard that the big man could not move.

"This game is good," said White Weasel. "Who will wrestle me next?" But no one came forward.

The two who pretended to be his parents stood to one side, talking.

"My son," said the man, "it is late. Tomorrow we will play a better game. We will go out to the little island at dawn and play ball with you."

"Come and spend the night in our lodge," said the woman.

"No," said the boy, "I am used to sleeping in the forest."

As White Weasel and Mikumwesu walked toward the forest, the man who pretended to be White Weasel's father called to the dog. "Bad Dog," he said, "come to me." But White Weasel's dog only growled and followed his master into the forest, where White Weasel and Mikumwesu built a fire and made camp.

That night there were many strange sounds in the forest around them. Four times the noises came very close. Each time, Bad Dog ran growling into the darkness and returned with blood on his teeth.

At dawn White Weasel and Mikumwesu went back to the village. The people of the village were waiting. Many of them were limping and had wounds on their arms and legs.

"My son," said the man who pretended to be White Weasel's father, "ride with me in our canoe."

Mikumwesu took White Weasel aside. "They will drown you if you ride with them. I will make a better canoe." The little man went down to the shore to a big white stone. He turned it over and shaped it into a canoe, then pushed it out onto the water. When he got inside, there was a paddle in his hands. White Weasel and Bad Dog climbed in with him, and the people of the village followed in their canoes of birch bark. Soon they reached the little island.

"Our ball field is on the other side of this island," said the one who pretended to be White Weasel's father. "Leave your dog here. No dogs can come to our ball field."

Again Mikumwesu spoke softly to White Weasel. "Great friend, these bad people will kill you when you reach the other side. Follow them till you reach the middle of the island, then turn around and run back here as quick as you can."

White Weasel set out, always staying a little behind the people of the village as they laughed and joked.

"This boy will never see another ball game better than ours," they said.

White Weasel kept stopping to tie one moccasin string and then the other. When the bad people were far ahead, he turned and ran as quick as he could back to the canoe and jumped in. He and Mikumwesu began to paddle.

"Look back," said the little man.

White Weasel looked back. The bad people were running down to their canoes. They no longer were disguised as human beings. Now he could see they were monsters.

Mikumwesu stood in the canoe and faced north.

"Grandfather," he called, "blow this island away."

Then a great wind came out of the north. It blew and it blew. When it stopped blowing, the island and the bad people were gone and were never seen again.

When they reached the mainland, Mikumwesu spoke to White Weasel.

"Great friend," he said, "I must go back to my wife. Return to your grandparents. Good things will happen now that the bad people have been swept away."

White Weasel and his dog walked south for many days. When they reached home, things were not as before. There were many lodges and many people who welcomed him and took him to the lodge of his grandparents.

"Grandson," said Fisher, "you have become a tall man."

"Grandson," said Wolverine, "now that the bad ones are gone and their village grown over with sumacs, your relatives have returned."

So White Weasel was reunited with his people. He became their chief and all went well for many years, and it was still going well when I left them.

Racing the Great Bear
Iroquois

Ne *onendji.* Hear my story, which happened long
ago. For many generations, the five nations of the
Haudenosaunee, the People of the Longhouse, had been
at war with one another. No one could say how the
wars began, but each time a man of one nation was
killed, his relatives sought revenge in the blood feud,
and so the fighting continued. Then the Creator took
pity on his people and sent a messenger of peace. The
Peacemaker traveled from nation to nation, convinc-
ing the people of the Five Nations—the Mohawk, the
Oneida, the Onondaga, the Cayuga, and the Seneca—
that it was wrong for brothers to kill one another. It was
not easy, but finally the nations agreed and the Great
Peace began. Most welcomed that peace, though there
were some beings with bad hearts who wished to see
the return of war.

One day, not long after the Great Peace had been
established, some young men in a Seneca village decided they would pay a visit to the Onondaga people.

"It is safe now to walk the trail between our nations,"
the young men said. "We will return after the sun has
risen and set seven times."

Then they set out. They walked toward the east until
they were lost from sight in the hills. But many more
than seven days passed, and those young men never
returned. Now another group of young men left, want-
ing to find out where their friends had gone. They, too,
did not return.

The people grew worried. Parties were sent out to
look for the vanished young men, but no sign was

found. And the searchers who went too far into the hills did not return, either.

The old chief of the village thought long and hard. He asked the clan mothers, those wise women whose job it was to choose the chiefs and give them good advice, what should be done.

"We must find someone brave enough to face whatever danger is out there," the clan mothers said.

So the old chief called the whole village to a council meeting. He held up a white strand of wampum beads made from quahog clamshells as he spoke.

"Hear me," he said. "I am of two minds about what has happened to our people. It may be that the Onondaga have broken the peace and captured them. It may be there is something with an evil mind that wishes to destroy this new peace and so has killed our people. Now someone must go and find out. Who is brave enough? Who will come and take this wampum from my hand?"

Many men were gathered in that council. Some were known to speak of themselves as brave warriors. Still, though they muttered to one another, no man stepped forward to take the strand of wampum. The old chief began to walk about the circle, holding the wampum in front of each man in turn. But each man only lowered his eyes to the ground. No man lifted his hand to take the wampum.

Just outside the circle stood a boy who had not yet become a man. His parents were dead, and he lived with his grandmother in her old lodge at the edge of the village. His clothing was always torn and his face dirty because his grandmother was too old to care for him as a mother would. The other young men made fun of him, and as a joke they called him Swift Runner—even though no one had ever seen him run and it was thought that he was weak and lazy. All he ever seemed to do was play with his little dog or sit by the fire and listen when the old people were talking.

"Our chief has forgotten our greatest warrior," one of the young men said to another, tilting his head toward Swift Runner.

"*Nyoh*," the other young man said, laughing. "Yes. Why does he not offer the wampum to Swift Runner?"

The chief looked around the circle of men, and the laughing stopped. He walked out of the circle to the place where the small boy in torn clothes stood. He held out the wampum and Swift Runner took it without hesitating.

"I accept this," Swift Runner said. "It is right that I be the one to face the danger. In the eyes of the people I am worthless, so if I do not return, it will not matter. I will leave when the sun rises tomorrow."

When Swift Runner arrived home at his grandmother's lodge, the old woman was waiting for him.

"Grandson," she said, "I know what you have done. The people of this village no longer remember, but your father was a great warrior. Our family is a family that has power."

Then she reached up into the rafters and took down a heavy bow. It was blackened with smoke and seemed so thick that no man could bend it.

"If you can string this bow, Grandson," the old woman said, "you are ready to face whatever waits for you on the trail."

Swift Runner took the bow. It was as thick as a man's wrist, but he bent it with ease and strung it.

"Wah-hah!" said his grandmother. "You are the one I knew you would grow up to be. Now you must sleep. At dawn we will make you ready for your journey."

It was not easy for Swift Runner to sleep, but when he woke the next morning, he felt strong and clear-headed. His grandmother was sitting by the fire with a cap in her hand.

"This was your grandfather's cap," she said. "I have sewed four hummingbird feathers on it. It will make your feet more swift."

Swift Runner took the cap and placed it on his head.

His grandmother held up four pairs of moccasins. "Carry these tied to your waist. When one pair wears out, throw them aside and put on the next pair."

Swift Runner took the moccasins and tied them to his belt.

Next his grandmother picked up a small pouch. "In this pouch is cornmeal mixed with maple sugar," she said. "It is the only food you will need as you travel. It will give you strength when you eat it each evening."

Swift Runner took the pouch and hung it from his belt by the moccasins.

"The last thing I must give you," said the old woman, "is this advice. Pay close attention to your little dog. You have treated him well and so he is your great friend. He is small, but his eyes and nose are keen. Keep him always in front of you. He will warn you of danger before it can strike you."

Then Swift Runner set out on his journey. His little dog stayed ahead of him, sniffing the air and sniffing the ground. By the time the sun was in the middle of the sky, they were far from the village. The trail passed through deep woods, and it seemed to the boy as if something was following them among the trees. But he could see nothing in the thick brush.

The trail curved toward the left, and the boy felt even more the presence of something watching. Suddenly his little dog ran into the brush at the side of the trail, barking loudly. There were the sounds of tree limbs breaking and heavy feet running. Then out of the forest came a Nyagwahe, a monster bear. Its great teeth were as long as a man's arm. It was twice as tall as a moose. Close at its heels was Swift Runner's little dog.

"I see you," Swift Runner shouted. "I am after you. You cannot escape me."

Swift Runner had learned those words by listening to the stories the old people told. They were the very words a monster bear speaks when it attacks, words that terrify anyone who hears them. On hearing those words, the great bear turned and fled from the boy.

"You cannot escape me," Swift Runner shouted again. Then he ran after the bear.

The Nyagwahe turned toward the east, with Swift Runner and his dog close behind. It left the trail and plowed through the thick forest, breaking down great trees and leaving a path of destruction like that of a whirlwind. It ran up the tallest hills and down through the swamps, but the boy and the dog stayed at its heels. They ran past a great cave in the rocks. All around the cave were the bones of people the bear had caught and eaten.

"My relatives," Swift Runner called as he passed the cave, "I will not forget you. I am after the one who killed you. He will not escape me."

Throughout the day, the boy and his dog chased the great bear, growing closer bit by bit. At last, as the sun began to set, Swift Runner stopped at the head of a small valley and called his small dog to him.

"We will rest here for the night," the boy said. He took off his first pair of moccasins, whose soles were worn away to nothing. He threw them aside and put on a new pair. Swift Runner made a fire and sat beside it with his dog. Then he took out the pouch of cornmeal and maple sugar, sharing his food with his dog.

"Nothing will harm us," Swift Runner said. "Nothing can come close to our fire." He lay down and slept.

In the middle of the night, he was awakened by the growling of his dog. He sat up with his back to the fire and looked into the darkness. There, just outside the circle of light made by the flames, stood a dark figure that looked like a tall man. Its eyes glowed green.

"I am Nyagwahe," said the figure. "This is my human shape. Why do you pursue me?"

"You cannot escape me," Swift Runner said. "I chase you because you killed my people. I will not stop until I catch you and kill you."

The figure faded back into the darkness.

"You cannot escape me," Swift Runner said again. Then he patted his small dog and went to sleep.

As soon as the first light of the new day appeared, Swift Runner rose. He and his small dog took the trail. It was easy to follow the monster's path, for trees were uprooted and the earth torn by its great paws. They ran all through the morning. When the sun was in the middle of the sky, they reached the head of another valley. At the other end they saw the great bear running toward the east. Swift Runner pulled off his second pair of moccasins, whose soles were worn away to nothing. He put on his third pair and began to run again.

All through that day, they kept the Nyagwahe in sight, drawing closer bit by bit. When the sun began to set, Swift Runner stopped to make camp. He took off the third pair of moccasins, whose soles were worn away to nothing, and put on the last pair.

"Tomorrow," he said to his small dog, "we will catch the monster and kill it." He reached for his pouch of cornmeal and maple sugar, but when he opened it, he found it filled with worms. The magic of the Nyagwahe had done this. Swift Runner poured out the pouch and said in a loud voice, "You have spoiled our food, but it will not stop me. I am on your trail. You cannot escape me."

That night, once again, he was awakened by the growling of his dog. A dark figure stood just outside the circle of light. It looked smaller than the night before, and the glow of its eyes was weak.

"I am Nyagwahe," the dark figure said. "Why do you pursue me?"

"You cannot escape me," Swift Runner said. "I am on your trail. You killed my people. You threatened the Great Peace. I will not rest until I catch you."

"Hear me," said the Nyagwahe. "I see your power is greater than mine. Do not kill me. When you catch me, take my great teeth. They are my power, and you can use them for healing. Spare my life and I will go far to the north and never again bother the People of the Longhouse."

"You cannot escape me," Swift Runner said. "I am on your trail."

The dark figure faded back into the darkness, and Swift Runner sat for a long time, looking into the night.

At the first light of day, the boy and his dog took the

trail. They had not gone far when they saw the Nyag-wahe ahead of them. Its sides puffed in and out as it ran. The trail was beside a big lake with many alder trees close to the water. As the great bear ran past, the leaves were torn from the trees. Fast as the bear went, the boy and his dog came closer, bit by bit. At last, when the sun was in the middle of the sky, the giant bear could run no longer. It fell heavily to the earth, panting so hard that it stirred up clouds of dust.

Swift Runner unslung his grandfather's bow and notched an arrow to the sinewy string.

"Shoot for my heart," said the Nyagwahe. "Aim well. If you cannot kill me with one arrow, I will take your life."

"No," Swift Runner said. "I have listened to the stories of my elders. Your only weak spot is the sole of your foot. Hold up your foot and I will kill you."

The great bear shook with fear. "You have defeated me," it pleaded. "Spare my life and I will leave forever."

"You must give me your great teeth," Swift Runner said. "Then you must leave and never bother the People of the Longhouse again."

"I shall do as you say," said the Nyagwahe. "Take my great teeth."

Swift Runner lowered his bow. He stepped forward and pulled out the great bear's teeth. It rose to its feet and walked to the north, growing smaller as it went. It went over the hill and was gone.

Carrying the teeth of the Nyagwahe over his shoulder, Swift Runner turned back to the west, his dog at his side. He walked for three moons before he reached the place where the bones of his people were piled in front of the monster's empty cave. He collected those bones and walked around them four times. "Now," he said, "I must do something to make my people wake up." He went to a big hickory tree and began to push it over so that it would fall on the pile of bones.

"My people," he shouted, "get up quickly or this tree will land on you."

The bones of the people who had been killed all came together and jumped up, alive again and covered with flesh. They were filled with joy and gathered around Swift Runner.

"Great one," they said, "who are you?"

"I am Swift Runner," he said.

"How can that be?" one of the men said. "Swift Runner is a skinny little boy. You are a tall, strong man."

Swift Runner looked at himself and saw that it was so. He was taller than the tallest man, and his little dog was bigger than a wolf.

"I am Swift Runner," he said. "I was that boy and I am the man you see before you."

Then Swift Runner led his people back to the village. He carried with him the teeth of the Nyagwahe, and those who saw what he carried rejoiced. The trails were safe again, and the Great Peace would not be broken. Swift Runner went to his grandmother's lodge and embraced her.

"Grandson," she said, "you are now the man I knew you would grow up to be. Remember to use your power to help the people."

So it was that Swift Runner ran with the great bear and won the race. Throughout his long life, he used the teeth of the Nyagwahe to heal the sick, and he worked always to keep the Great Peace.

Da neho. I am finished.

Granny Squannit and the
Bad Young Man
Wampanoag

Long ago, Tooquahmi Squannit lived in a cave near the sand dunes at Cummaquid. Granny Squannit was an old, old woman. She was short and strong, and she wore her long black hair over her face so that only her mouth could be seen. She avoided other people most of the time and knew a great deal about medicine. Even though Granny Squannit lived away from the village at Nauset, she always seemed to know all of the things that were going on with the people. She was especially interested in the children. If a child misbehaved, she might appear suddenly in front of that child to frighten him. It was said that any child who had seen Granny Squannit was always good after that.

In those days, when a boy reached a certain age, it was the custom for him to go through a special initiation to prepare himself to become a man. That boy would be blindfolded and taken out deep into the forest by his uncle to a place where he was expected to stay for three moons. He was given nothing to help take care of himself. While he was gone he would have to build his own shelter and gather his own food. The boy was supposed to think deeply about the responsibility of being a man and caring for the people. This vigil in the forest was not an easy thing to do, but every boy who wished to become a man would do it.

One boy, however, refused to do as his elders suggested. When the time came for him to go alone into the forest, he said no. This boy always thought of himself first and not of others. He would not listen to advice from others. He showed no respect to his elders, even his own grandparents. It seemed as if a bad spirit had gotten into his heart, and there was no way to stop his bad behavior. His father spoke to him, but the boy did not change. His uncle spoke to him, but the boy ignored him. His grandfather spoke to him, but the boy paid no attention. Even the sachem, the old chief of the village, spoke to the boy, but it had no effect. In fact, if that boy was not watched every minute, he would destroy things.

"Where is our son?" his father asked one day.

"I do not know," his mother said, "but I smell something burning."

"Ah-ah! He has made a fire behind the lodge and is burning my arrows!"

The boy was taken to the *pauwau*, the wise old man who was able to cure diseases of the spirit and see deep into the heart of any sickness. The old man looked into the boy's face. He tried his strongest medicines, but they did not touch the badness that held on to the boy's heart. As soon as the *pauwau* turned his back, the boy grabbed the old man's wampum belts and ran down and threw them over the cliff into the ocean.

"There is nothing I can do," the *pauwau* said. "He is a bad young man."

And so that became the boy's name among the people: Bad Young Man. From that time on, no one called him by any other name.

One day, Bad Young Man followed some of the younger children down to the river. As soon as they got there, he began to push them into the water. But as he was doing this, a canoe came up the river. Even though the person in the canoe was not paddling, it cut its way swiftly upstream. And the person in the canoe was Granny Squannit, her long black hair over her face.

The other children climbed up onto the bank and ran, but Bad Young Man stood there in the water, unable to move. Granny Squannit's canoe came right up to him. Then the old woman reached out her arm and yanked him into the canoe. The canoe turned around and went swiftly down the river. Soon it was close to the ocean, near Cummaquid where the sand dunes rose. Granny Squannit pulled her canoe up onto the sand and then yanked Bad Young Man out of the canoe. She held him so hard by the arm that he could not pull away. She took him straight into her cave and sat him down.

Bad Young Man wanted to run away, but he could not move. Granny Squannit came to him with a bowl of green soup in her hand. She gave it to Bad Young Man, and even though he did not want to, he drank it all. And he fell asleep.

When he woke up, four days had passed. He looked around the cave. Where was the old woman who had brought him here? Then he saw Granny Squannit. She was lying across the mouth of the cave and she seemed to be asleep, her long black hair over her face.

If I am very quiet, he thought, I can sneak out and get away from her.

Carefully, quietly, he crawled toward the entrance of the cave. Carefully, quietly, he stepped over the old woman as she slept. But as he was about to leave, he became curious. No one had ever seen Granny Squannit's face. Bad Young Man turned back, leaned over, and pushed the hair away from the old woman's face so he could see what she really looked like. There, staring up at him was—not two eyes, but one! One huge, wide-open eye was there in the center of Granny Squannit's face. It seemed as if that eye were looking straight into the center of his spirit. The boy shouted and fell back against the wall of the cave.

Granny Squannit stood up. She could see that the badness had been frightened out of the boy. She pushed the hair in front of her face and took him by the arm, gently this time, to lead him back into the cave. She took out a deerskin pouch, placed roots and other medicine plants into it, and sewed it shut. Then she gave it to the boy.

"Wear this about your neck," Granny Squannit said. "It will remind you to keep goodness in your heart."

The boy did as she said. He returned to his people and was a bad young man no longer. Before long, he gained a new name. He became known as High Eagle. High Eagle respected his elders and did things with other people in mind. He continued to do good things and gained more respect, until one day High Eagle became Grand Sachem of his people.

THE SOUTHEAST

Perhaps more than those of people in any other section of North America, the lives of the Native peoples of the Southeast were disrupted by the coming of the Europeans. The Cherokee and Creek peoples were among the five nations that became known as the Five Civilized Tribes for their outward adoption of European ways. Despite the removal of most of the Cherokee and Creek peoples to Oklahoma, their cultures have shown great resilience. Farther to the west, at the southeastern edge of the plains, the Caddo and Osage peoples also found themselves forced to relocate to Oklahoma.

As a result of these forced migrations, the Native peoples of the Southeast, including those who have managed to remain in their original homelands, are often overlooked. This is a great shame, for they have not disappeared and—as the following stories show— they still have much to teach us all.

The ecological balance of things is important in

Native American traditions. If people behave correctly, nature will provide all that is needed. The Cherokee legend "How the Game Animals Were Set Free," one story exemplifying this belief, is both humorous and instructive. Learning in Native American cultures is usually through experience. Instead of being told how to behave, a child is allowed to make mistakes and then learns from the consequences.

On the other hand, that kind of freedom also permits a child to discover his or her own power. In the Caddo tale "The Wild Boy," the twins become powerful beings through their quest. As is the case in many Native stories, a wise parent lets the natural world teach the lesson through experience.

The highest ideal in these cultures, and in most of the cultures of Native North America, is not to achieve personal wealth but to gain the knowledge and the power that will enable individuals to serve their people. A high degree of individual freedom carries with it an equally large responsibility to the community. In the Creek story "The Underwater Lodge," Blue Fox fails to discharge properly his duty to his father. He risks his life in the domain of the fearful tie-snakes until he understands the meaning of freedom and responsibility.

The Osage also believed in living in harmony with nature. They were among the tallest of the people of the southeastern plains, yet they saw that they were small compared with the land around them and the greatness of Wah-Kon-Tah, the Great Mystery. So they called themselves the Little Ones.

The Osage divided themselves into two groups, the Honga (the People of the Earth) and the Tzi-sho (the

People of the Sky). Each of the many Osage clans was guided by the nonhuman beings around it—a plant, an animal, or even a star. "The Wisdom of the Willow Tree" is one such story of how a new symbol of wisdom and strength was given to a young man of the Earth People.

How the Game Animals Were Set Free
Cherokee

Long ago, at the foot of Looking-Glass Mountain, there lived a hunter named Kanati and his two sons, First Boy and Inage Utasuhi'. Inage Utasuhi', whose name meant "The Boy Who Grew Up Wild," was always getting himself and his brother into trouble.

Each day Kanati, whose name meant "The Lucky Hunter," would go out to get game for them to eat, and each day he was successful. First Boy and Inage Utasuhi' would stay behind and play hunting games together.

"Take us with you," Inage Utasuhi' would ask each day, but Kanati refused.

"You are not yet old enough to hunt. If you are not ready and you try to hunt, then bad things may happen. If you are not serious when you hunt, bad things will happen. When you are ready, I will take you with me."

The boys listened at first, but one morning when Kanati left the lodge, Inage Utasuhi' spoke to his brother. "Let us follow our father and watch what he does. How else can we learn to be men?"

The two boys set out, following their father but keeping back so he would not see them. Before long, Kanati came to a hollow tree. The boys could not see what he was doing.

"I will go closer," said Inage Utasuhi'. Then he changed himself into a small bird and flew to a branch of the hollow tree.

Kanati reached into the tree and pulled out a bundle covered in deerskin. When he unwrapped it, Inage Utasuhi' could see that there was something strange inside. It was a long, bent stick with a piece of strong cord made of milkweed fibers fastened from one end of it to the other. Then Kanati placed the deerskin wrappings in the hollow tree and began to walk. As he walked, he plucked the string and it made a humming sound.

Inage Utasuhi' flew back to First Boy and turned into a human again.

"I do not know what our father is doing," the wild boy said. "But if we wish to learn how to hunt, we must follow him and watch."

So the boys continued to follow Kanati. Soon he came to a swampy place where many reeds grew. Before their father went in among the reeds, Inage Utasuhi' spoke to his brother.

"Wait here," he said. "I will go and see what he does." Then the wild boy changed himself into a downy feather, floated through the wind, and landed unseen on Kanati's shoulder. In the shape of the downy feather, the wild boy watched closely as Kanati selected and cut the straightest reed. He reached into his pouch and took out a goose feather. He split it with his flint knife and then tied it with sinew to the reed. He cut a notch in one end of the reed and sharpened the other end. Then Kanati took the long, feathered reed and fitted it to the string of the bent stick he carried.

When Kanati returned from the reeds, the wind blew the downy feather off his shoulder. It floated back and forth in the air as the hunter walked away, and then, as soon as it touched the ground, turned into Inage Utasuhi'.

First Boy came out of the bushes where he had been hiding and joined his brother.

"We are learning a great deal," the wild boy said. "Let us continue to follow and see what our father does."

Before long, Kanati came to the side of Looking-Glass

Mountain. There was a cave, blocked by a big stone. Kanati rolled the stone away from the mouth of the cave, and a big deer came running out. Kanati raised the bow and shot his arrow, killing the deer. Then he rolled the stone in front of the cave, picked up his deer, and headed toward home.

"If we want to be men," Inage Utasuhi' said, "we must do as our father did."

So the two boys went back and cut saplings to make bows. They made cordage from milkweed fibers and strung their bows. They went into the reeds and cut the straightest ones. Then each of the boys made seven arrows.

"Now we are ready to hunt," said Inage Utasuhi'. He led his brother to the cave, and together they rolled away the stone. Immediately a big deer ran out. It came out so fast that the boys were too surprised to shoot. The wild boy struck at it with one of the arrows in his hand, but he only hit the deer's tail, knocking it straight up. The deer bounded off into the forest with the white of its tail showing above its back.

"Oho, brother, did you see that?" Inage Utasuhi' said, laughing. "See if you can do the same."

Another deer ran out and First Boy struck at its tail with his arrow. As soon as he knocked the tail, it stood straight up and stayed there as the deer ran away. Both boys laughed. This was great fun. For a long time, they took turns striking at each deer as it ran out, until all the deer had left the cave. Ever since then, all deer have tails that stick straight up when they run.

Other game animals began to come out of the cave. The boys watched them. Soon, so many were running out that Inage Utasuhi' and First Boy became afraid.

They tried to move the stone back, but the animals were too fast and too many. Rabbits and raccoons and squirrels and possums and all of the four-legged animals came out while the boys just watched. Then birds flew out in great numbers. There were turkeys and grouse and pigeons and all the other birds that people hunted. They came out in flocks so large, they darkened the sky and their wings were like the rumble of thunder. Now the boys grew frightened, but they could not roll the stone into the mouth of the cave.

Back in his lodge, Kanati heard the rumbling sound. He looked up and saw the sky was dark with birds.

"Oho," he said, "what are my bad boys doing?" He left the lodge quickly and hurried to the cave. Fast as Kanati ran, he was not fast enough. By the time he came to the place where he had kept the game animals and the birds, all of them had escaped. The two boys were still standing there, watching.

Kanati said nothing. But he knew that his boys needed to be punished for their deed. He went into the cave and brought out four clay pots. Putting them down, he knocked the lid off each one. Biting insects came flying out and landed on the two boys. Though Inage Utasuhi' and First Boy swatted and jumped, they could not rid themselves of the fleas and flies, the gnats and mosquitoes. At last Kanati thought they had been punished enough. He brushed the insects off the boys. But the insects did not go back into the pots. They went out and spread all over the world. And to this day, there are still fleas and flies and gnats and mosquitoes.

"You have not done well," Kanati said to the boys. "It will no longer be easy for us to hunt. Had you done as I said and waited until you were ready, the game animals would not have been freed. A hunter must always be serious and show respect for the animals. You were not serious as you hunted, and so all the game animals escaped. You have learned how to make bows and arrows, and they will be needed from now on. No longer can we be sure that we will bring home game animals to eat. Now we will have to work hard to hunt the animals, and even then we cannot be sure of success."

And so, because of what Kanati's sons did back then, it is still that way to this day.

The Wild Boy
Caddo

There was a hunter who lived with his wife and their son, a boy twelve winters old, in a lodge near a stream deep in the woods. Because this hunter was wise in the ways of healing and plants, he was called Medicine Person. Each day, when he came home with the game he had killed, his wife would take it down to the stream to wash the blood away.

One day, when the hunter returned carrying a large deer, his wife was gone. Their son was sitting in the back of the lodge. He looked frightened and tired.

"Where is your mother?" Medicine Person said.

"I do not know," Lodge Boy answered. "She went to the spring to get water, and I heard a scream and a terrible noise. I ran there and called for her many times, but she did not return."

Medicine Person and Lodge Boy searched a long time for her. All they could find were some of her torn clothes and the tracks of a large animal leading away to the west. With great sorrow, the hunter accepted that his wife was dead. Together he and his son built a fire and kept it burning for six days as they sat beside it in mourning. On the seventh day, Medicine Person went hunting again.

"My son," Medicine Person said as he left, "do not go far from our lodge when I am away."

"Can I go down to the stream and play?" the boy asked.

"Yes," Medicine Person said, "but go no farther than that."

Each day for many days after that, when Medicine Person came home, he found his son waiting for him.

One evening, however, Medicine Person returned from hunting by a different trail than the one he usually took. When he reached the lodge, his son was not there. But as he listened carefully, he heard the sound of voices coming from the direction of the stream. Medicine Person did not take the trail but crept down to the stream through the brush. When he looked out, he saw his son and another boy talking and playing. The other boy was about his son's size and resembled him, except that the other boy had long, tangled hair and a long nose. As soon as Medicine Person stepped out of his hiding place, the other boy leaped into the stream and was gone.

"Who are you playing with?" Medicine Person asked his son. "Who are his parents and where does he live?"

"Father," Lodge Boy said, "my friend does not have a name, and he lives in the forest. He says that his mother is my mother, but she came here to the stream and threw him away."

As soon as he heard those words, Medicine Person understood. This wild boy had sprung from the blood of the deer that his wife always washed in the stream.

"My son," Medicine Person said, "we must bring your brother into our lodge. It is not right that he should have to live alone in the forest."

"That will not be easy, Father. I have tried to bring him to our lodge before, but he says he must remain in the forest and not be tamed. He always runs away when he hears you coming home because he says that you will make him live like a human being."

"Tomorrow," Medicine Person said, "I will only pretend to go hunting. I will turn myself into a cricket and hide here by the side of the lodge. Bring your brother close and I will jump out and grab him."

The next day Medicine Person turned himself into a cricket and hid while Lodge Boy went down to the stream. Soon the boy came back up the trail with his brother beside him. But as soon as Wild Boy saw the cricket by the side of the lodge, he stopped.

"Who is that man hiding behind the lodge?" Wild Boy asked. Then he turned and ran away.

The next day Medicine Person tried again. "I will make myself into a stick and hide in the roof of the lodge. Bring your brother close and I will catch him."

Just as before, Wild Boy came within sight of the lodge and stopped. "Who is that man hiding in the roof?" he asked, looking at the stick. Then he ran away.

Each day Medicine Person tried another hiding place. Each day Wild Boy saw him and ran away. Finally, on the night before the seventh day, Medicine Person left Lodge Boy by their lodge and went to a little clearing in the forest. At the edge of the clearing, he made a small shelter covered with grass and leaves so that it could not easily be seen. Then he returned to their lodge and spoke to his son.

"Tomorrow we must catch your brother, for I will have used up all of my powers. You must do as I say. Take Wild Boy to the clearing west of our lodge. I will leave a fire burning there. Sit him by the fire and tell him that you wish to comb out his hair. As you do so, knot his hair four times and hold on to it and call me."

This time Medicine Person did not let Lodge Boy know where he was going to hide. Soon, from his hiding place, he heard the sound of the boys approaching.

"Brother," Lodge Boy said, "let me comb the tangles out of your hair."

Wild Boy looked around but could see no one. He sat

down by the fire and turned his back to his brother. As soon as Lodge Boy had made four knots in the hair of Wild Boy, he held on and called out, "Father, we are ready."

Then Medicine Person jumped out of the fire where he had been hiding and grabbed hold of Wild Boy. He took him to the little shelter covered with grass and leaves and placed him and his brother inside it for six days. On the seventh day, he brought the boys out. Lodge Boy washed his brother clean, and Medicine Person took his knife and cut off the long end of Wild Boy's nose. The two boys looked like twins.

Medicine Person said to Wild Boy, "You have been playing with my son and calling him your brother. Now you are brothers indeed. Stay in our lodge and play with him while I am gone."

Medicine Person went off to hunt. But before he left, he told his boys not to go toward the west, for there were giant squirrels there that killed and ate children.

However, even though he now looked like his brother, it was still Wild Boy's nature to do things his own way. As soon as Medicine Person was out of sight, Wild Boy picked up his bow and arrows.

"Brother," he said, "let us walk toward the west."

The two brothers walked and walked until they came to a place in the forest where the trees were very tall. In one of the trees was a big hollow and, in that hollow, the giant squirrels lived.

"We will stay far away from the tree, and the giant squirrels will not be able to reach us," Wild Boy said. But even as he spoke, one of the giant squirrels poked out its head and saw the boys. It opened its mouth and a long tongue, longer than the tongue of a frog, flicked out and caught Lodge Boy. Before Wild Boy could do anything, the giant squirrel had swallowed his brother and disappeared back into the tree. Without saying anything, Wild Boy turned and walked home. When he went into the lodge, his father was there, home from hunting.

"Where is your brother?" Medicine Person asked.

"He is waiting for me in the forest. We are making arrows. I came home to get fire so that we could heat the shafts to straighten them," Wild Boy answered. He picked up a burning brand from the fire and left.

When he reached the place in the forest where the tall trees grew and the giant squirrels lived, Wild Boy made a big fire using the burning brand. He gathered red stones and placed them in the fire until they were white with heat.

Then he picked up the stones with peeled green branches and threw them into the hollow tree. Smoke began to pour out of the tree. Finally the giant squirrel came crawling from the hole and fell dead on the ground. Wild Boy turned it over and cut open its stomach. Out crawled Lodge Boy, unharmed.

"Do not tell our father what happened," Wild Boy said. "If he finds out, he will not let us play anymore."

"Brother, you are right," Lodge Boy said. Then the brothers went back home. When they arrived at the lodge, Medicine Person was waiting for them but said nothing. So the two brothers were able to continue to play together.

The next day, Medicine Person spoke to his sons. "While I am gone, stay close to the lodge. Do not go to the west, for that is where the ones who eat human beings live. They are the ones who killed your mother."

The two boys waited until their father had left and then began to play the game of shooting at the hoop. They had made a hoop of elm bark, and each boy would take a turn rolling it while the other boy shot at it, trying to stop it with his arrows.

Wild Boy, however, soon tired of the game. He made two magical arrows, one black and one blue, and gave them to his brother.

"Use these arrows for our game," he said. Then Wild Boy rolled the hoop. Each time the hoop was rolled, Lodge Boy shot one of the magic arrows and struck the hoop, stopping it.

"Roll it faster, brother," Lodge Boy said. "This is too easy."

Wild Boy blew on the hoop to fill it, too, with magic power. He rolled the hoop as hard as he could. It went past Lodge Boy so fast that he did not shoot, and it rolled toward the western horizon, where it seemed to go up into the sky as it went out of sight.

"We have lost our hoop," Lodge Boy said sadly.

"Do not worry, brother," Wild Boy said. "We will be able to go where it has gone and find it." He picked up a buffalo-calf robe that Medicine Person had tanned, draped it over his shoulders, and began to walk.

The two boys walked together toward the horizon. They walked for a long time, following the track made by the hoop as it rolled across the ground. When it was midday, Wild Boy stopped, for the track of the hoop had ended.

"Here is the place where our hoop has gone up into the sky," he said. "Now I must go up and follow it." He reached into his pouch and brought out two nuts from the pecan tree. Placing one in the earth, he spoke a few words. Immediately a pecan tree burst up from the soil. It grew taller and taller, high into the sky.

"You must be ready to help me," Wild Boy said. "I am going to climb up to the top. Do not watch me as I climb, but continue always to look down at the earth. I will be gone a long time. You will know when I have reached the top, for my bones will begin to fall back to the ground. You must wait till all of them have fallen and gather them together. Cover them with this buffalo-calf robe. Shoot the blue arrow into the robe and call on me to stand up."

Wild Boy began to climb the tree. Up and up he went as Lodge Boy sat at the base of the tree, looking always at the ground. A long time passed, but Lodge Boy did not look up. Then a small bone fell on the ground beside him. More and more bones fell around him, until he was certain that all of Wild Boy's bones were there. He gathered the bones together, covered them with the robe, and drew back his arrow.

"Brother," he shouted, "stand up now!" He fired the blue arrow into the buffalo-calf robe, and when it struck, Wild Boy was standing there next to the robe. He was much the same as before, yet there was something different about him.

"Our Great Father has given me much power," Wild Boy said. "Now you must climb up, too, and you will be given power." He sat down by the big pecan tree and stared at the ground as Lodge Boy climbed. After a long time, Lodge Boy's bones fell from the tree. When they had all fallen, Wild Boy gathered them and covered them with the buffalo-calf robe. He drew back the blue arrow and shouted, "Get up, brother, or this arrow will strike you." As soon as his arrow struck the robe, Lodge Boy was standing there.

"Tell me," Wild Boy said, "what happened to you?"

"I climbed so high," Lodge Boy said, "that I reached the top of the tree. I could see nothing, and it seemed as if I were dreaming. Then the Great Sky Father touched me, and I watched as my bones fell toward the earth. I heard you call to me and I stood up."

"That is how it was with me," Wild Boy said. "You, too, have been given great power. Let me see what kind of power you have."

Lodge Boy opened his mouth and a great sound, the rolling of thunder, filled the air.

"You are Thunder Boy now," said Wild Boy. "Let me test my power." He opened his mouth and lightning came from it.

"You are Lightning Boy," his brother said. "But we must return to our lodge, for our father will be worried."

"No," Lightning Boy said, "first we must find the track of our hoop and locate it. When I was up in the sky, I could see the place where it was brought back down to the earth by the one who called it into the sky. The one who took the hoop is dangerous, but our power will protect us now." He put the buffalo-calf robe over his shoulders. "Let us go."

The two brothers set out again. Before they had gone far, they found the track of the hoop in the earth. They walked a long way until they came to a very wide lake. The brothers could see no way around it.

"We must cross over," Lightning Boy said. "My power tells me that our hoop is on the other side."

He reached into his pouch and pulled out the second pecan nut. As he planted it, he spoke a few words and again a tall pecan tree burst up from the earth. But as this tree grew, it began to curve until its top touched the ground on the other side of the lake. The boys crossed over this bridge and again found the track of their hoop. However, after they followed it a short way, the trail ended. There, coming toward them, was a figure that Thunder Boy thought was an old man. The old man smiled at Thunder Boy and held up the elm-bark hoop he was carrying.

"That is not really an old man," Lightning Boy said. "My power tells me he is the evil one who stole our hoop and means to kill us. Use your power, brother."

Thunder Boy opened his mouth and the sound of thunder split the air. The old man stopped coming toward them and turned to run. Lightning Boy opened his mouth and lightning shot out, striking the old man. As the lightning hit and killed him, they saw he was not an old man at all, but a being shaped like a human with long, sharp teeth and long, clawed hands. He was a Man-Eater. Beside his body was the elm-bark hoop.

"We must follow his tracks," Lightning Boy said. "His village is close to here." Then Lightning Boy used his power again. He bent over, and when he straightened up he looked like an old man, just as the Man-Eater had. Thunder Boy walked behind his brother as they followed the old man's trail back toward the lake. Before long they saw a village and what appeared to be many people standing in the center of the town. However, when Thunder Boy used his power, he could see that these beings, too, had long, sharp teeth and long, clawed fingers. They were Man-Eaters.

When they saw the old man coming into the village leading the boy, the Man-Eaters became excited.

"Our chief has brought food," they shouted.

Then Lightning Boy stood up straight and no longer looked like an old man. "Use your power," he said to his brother.

Thunder Boy opened his mouth and the sound of thunder rolled over the land, knocking all of those in the village to the ground. Lightning Boy opened his mouth and lightning flashed out, killing all the Man-Eaters.

"Let us look through the bones of the people they ate," said Lightning Boy. They began to rummage through the piles of bones scattered about the village. There were bones of humans of all shapes and sizes. Thunder Boy lifted up a bone from one pile off to the side of the others. As soon as he did so, he heard a familiar voice saying, "My son, I am glad you have found me."

"These are the bones of our mother!" Thunder Boy said excitedly.

Thunder Boy and Lightning Boy gathered together all of their mother's bones and covered them with the buffalo-calf robe.

"Mother," the boys shouted, "get up or these arrows will strike you!" Before the arrows pierced the skin, their mother stood there, alive and well.

"My sons," she said, "I have been sleeping too long." Then she embraced both the boys.

The three of them walked back toward the east where Medicine Person's lodge stood. When they reached the clearing, they saw that grass and small trees had grown all around the lodge, and there was no sign of life. Although it had seemed that their journey took only a single day, they had been gone for many years. They had been gone so long that their father thought them dead.

"Father," the boys called. "We have returned. Our mother is with us."

Then Medicine Person came out of his lodge. He looked old and tired, but when he saw his wife and his sons, the weight of the years lifted from him and he stood straight again.

For many years after, Medicine Person and his wife lived together happily with their sons. But when their parents finally died, Thunder Boy and Lightning Boy wished to stay no longer on the earth. They went up into the sky and there they remain. And, to this very day, when the two brothers look down from the clouds and see evil beings planning to harm their people, the voice of Thunder Boy may be heard as Lightning Boy's bolts flash through the sky.

The Underwater Lodge
Muskogee (Creek)

Long ago, the Muskogee people lived in the southern land of many rivers. There were many towns of the Muskogee, and one of the largest was the town of Koweta. One day, the chief of Koweta called his son, Blue Fox, to him. Blue Fox was a slender youth who had not yet been initiated into manhood. He loved and respected his father, but like all boys he also loved to play with his friends. Often when his father looked for him, he would be playing ball or running through the woods or swimming down at the river with his friends. His father hoped that his son would learn the importance of responsibility so that someday he, too, might be chosen to serve the people as their chief.

"My son," he said one morning, "you are young, but you are a good runner. I wish you to take a message to the chief of the town of Talladega. Give him this bowl so he will recognize that the message you carry comes from me. This responsibility is great, and I trust you to do this well."

Blue Fox listened closely to the message and then took the bowl from his father's hands. He set out on the trail that ran along the Chattahoochee River. Before he had gone far, he saw some of his friends playing in the water.

"Blue Fox," they called, "come join us."

It was early in the day and there was plenty of time to deliver his message. Blue Fox went down by the water where his friends were floating boats they had made of sticks tied together. Blue Fox had no boat, but the bowl in his hands was shaped like a boat. He put the bowl in the water and it floated away from him toward the deep part of the river. It turned in a circle four times, and then sank.

Blue Fox was frightened. He could not carry his message without the bowl. He knew that the river was dangerous. It was said that there were tie-snakes, bright-colored creatures that would wrap themselves about swimmers who went into the deepest waters. Still, he was more afraid of disappointing his father. He swam to the place where the bowl had sunk.

"Blue Fox," his friends called, "be careful. The river is deep and the current is fast."

But Blue Fox did not listen. He dived down and he did not come up again. His friends waited for him until the sun was high overhead.

"Our friend has drowned," they said, and they went sadly back to Koweta town to tell the people of Blue Fox's death.

However, Blue Fox was not dead. As soon as he dived beneath the surface, many tie-snakes wrapped around him and carried the boy down to the very bottom of the river. When they set him free, he saw that he was in a cave.

"Climb up the s-stairs-s," the tie-snakes said.

Blue Fox looked at the stairs in front of him and saw they were made of living snakes all wrapped together. They were many colors: blue, yellow, red, white, and green. At the top of the stairs was a platform made of even more snakes. And on top of that platform sat a great tie-snake. Blue Fox knew immediately that the great snake must be the chief.

The chief of the tie-snakes wore a feathered headpiece and was black all over except for its throat, which was white. It had a hooked beak like a hawk's and its eyes glowed red as hot coals. Horns of brilliant blue and yellow grew from its head. Next to the great snake was the message bowl given to Blue Fox by his father.

Blue Fox tried to climb the steps, but as he lifted his foot, the steps moved and he stopped. It seemed to him that if he placed his foot upon the stairs, the snakes would tangle themselves about him and he would be crushed to death. He tried a second time. The stairs moved again, and he hesitated. He tried a third time and again pulled back as the stairs moved beneath him. Then he reminded himself of his responsibility. He had failed his father once, but he would not do it again. He placed his foot on the stairs and step-by-step climbed up to the place where the Chief of the Tie-Snakes sat.

"Welcome to my lodge. S-s-sit beside me," said the Tie-Snake Chief. The seat was made of living snakes, too. As Blue Fox approached, the eyes of those snakes followed him. It seemed that if he sat down, he would surely be killed. Blue Fox tried three times to sit. Then on the fourth try, he thought of the trust his father had placed in him. Only if he sat by the great snake would he have a chance to retrieve the message bowl he had been entrusted to carry. Blue Fox took a deep breath and sat down beside the great snake.

Then the chief pointed with its head toward a corner of the cave. "That feather is yours-s-s," said the Tie-Snake Chief.

Blue Fox went over to the tall feather. It was a heron plume like the ones on the great snake's headpiece. It seemed that there was so much power in the feather, it would burn him if he tried to touch it. But he reminded himself again of his responsibility. Three times he tried to grasp the feather, and three times its power was too great for his hand. On the fourth try, he said to himself, "I must be a man." Then he reached out and grasped the heron feather.

"You see that ax?" said the Tie-Snake Chief, motioning with its head toward another corner of the cave. "That ax is yours-s-s."

Blue Fox walked over to the ax and reached for it. It moved away from his hands and he could feel its power. He wondered if he was strong enough to hold it. Each time he reached, as he felt that uncertainty, the ax lifted itself above his grasp. But on the fourth try, he said to himself, "I am no longer a child; I am tall enough to reach this ax. I am strong enough to hold it." Then he reached for the ax and took it in his hand.

"You can return to your father now," said the Tie-Snake Chief. "Three days-s have passed in the world beneath the s-sky. He will as-s-k you where you have been. Tell him only 'I know what I know,' but do not tell him what you have learned. Do not tell him about the powerful things-s you have been given.

"S-soon you will need my help. You have proven yourself to be a young man who knows-s the meaning of res-spons-s-sibility. S-s-so I will help you. When you need my help, place my feather on your head. Walk to the eas-st and bow three times toward the ris-sing s-s-sun. I will come to help you."

Then the tie-snakes wrapped themselves around Blue Fox and carried him up to the surface of the water. As he stood on the bank, the tie-snakes dived back underwater and came up again with his father's message bowl. Blue Fox carried it to the village of the Talladega, where he placed it in the hands of the chief and delivered his message.

"We heard that you had drowned," said the Talladega chief. "Stay and tell us where you have been."

"I cannot say," Blue Fox said. "I must return to my father." Then he ran back to his village. When he walked into his house, his father welcomed him with joy.

"My son," the chief of Koweta said, embracing Blue Fox, "I thought you had drowned. Where have you been?"

"I have been with the tie-snakes. Their chief has instructed me to tell you only that I know what I know. I cannot tell you more," Blue Fox said.

Blue Fox's father looked at him. He could see that his son was not the same as he had been before. He seemed taller and straighter. Blue Fox had been touched by some power beyond that of human beings. So the chief accepted the words of his son and asked no further questions.

It was clear to the people of Koweta town, too, that Blue Fox was no longer the boy he had been. He carried with him the plume and the ax that the Tie-Snake Chief had given him, but would tell no one what they meant. His only answer to their questions was always, "I know what I know."

One day Blue Fox's father spoke to him. "My son, our scouts have brought a message. Our enemies from the lands of the Cherokee are coming to attack our village. There are many of them, and I am afraid they will kill us. Can you use what you know to help us?"

Blue Fox placed the feather on his head and took the ax in his hand. He walked down to the river, faced the rising sun, and bowed three times. When he raised his head after bowing the third time, the Tie-Snake Chief stood before him.

"My father needs your help," Blue Fox said.

"Tell him not to fear," the Tie-Snake Chief said. "Your enemies-s will attack, but all will be well." Then he was gone.

Blue Fox returned to Koweta town. By midday, the people heard the sound of many enemies coming. Soon a large band of Cherokee warriors was in sight walking along the bank of the river, ready to attack the town. Blue Fox raised his ax. As he did so, thousands of tie-snakes came crawling out of the water. They wrapped themselves around the feet of the enemy warriors until all of the attacking Cherokees lay on the ground, tangled in the coils of the tie-snakes.

Blue Fox approached them. "You must promise never to attack us again."

For a moment the Cherokees hesitated. But as Blue Fox raised his ax, all of the tie-snakes began to hiss and tighten their coils.

"We agree," said the captured warriors.

Once again, Blue Fox raised his ax. The tie-snakes uncoiled themselves and crawled to the side of the river bank.

The freed enemies looked at the snakes waiting near their feet and vowed even more strongly that they would always be friends of the Koweta. The power of Blue Fox was too great.

So it was that the Koweta were saved from their enemies. In time, just as his father had hoped, Blue Fox himself was chosen to be chief of the Koweta. And throughout his lifetime, his people lived in peace because of Blue Fox's visit to the underwater lodge of the Tie-Snake Chief.

The Wisdom of the Willow Tree
Osage

What is the meaning of life? Why is it that people grow old and die? Although he was young, those questions troubled the mind of Little One. He asked the elders about them, but their answers did not satisfy him. At last he knew there was only one thing to do. He would have to seek the answers in his dreams.

Little One rose early in the morning and prayed to Wah-Kon-Tah for help. Then he walked away from the village, across the prairie and toward the hills. He took nothing with him, no food or water. He was looking for a place where none of his people would see him, a place where a vision could come to him.

Little One walked a long way. Each night he camped in a different place, hoping that it would be the right one to give him a dream that could answer his questions. But no such dream came to him.

At last he came to a hill that rose above the land like the breast of a turkey. A spring burst from the rocks near the base of a great elm tree. It was such a beautiful place that it seemed to be filled with the power of Wah-Kon-Tah. Little One sat down by the base of that elm tree and waited as the sun set. But though he slept, again no sign was given to him.

When he woke the next morning, he was weak with hunger. I must go back home, he thought. He was filled with despair, but his thoughts were of his parents. He had been gone a long time. Even though it was expected that a young man would seek guidance alone in this fashion, Little One knew they would be worried.

"If I do not return while I still have the strength to

walk," he said, "I will die here and my family may never find my body."

So Little One began to follow the small stream that was fed by the spring. It flowed out of the hills in the direction of his village, and he trusted it to lead him home. He walked and walked until he was not far from his village. But as he walked along that stream, he stumbled and fell among the roots of an old willow tree.

Little One clung to the roots of the willow tree. Although he tried to rise, his legs were too weak.

"Grandfather," he said to the willow tree, "it is not possible for me to go on."

Then the ancient willow spoke to him.

"Little One," it said, "all the Little Ones always cling to me for support as they walk along the great path of life. See the base of my trunk, which sends forth those roots that hold me firm in the earth. They are the sign of my old age. They are darkened and wrinkled with age, but they are still strong. Their strength comes from relying on the earth. When the Little Ones use me as a symbol, they will not fail to see old age as they travel along the path of life."

Those words gave strength to Little One's spirit. He stood again and began to walk. Soon his own village was in sight, and as he sat down to rest for a moment in the grass of the prairie, looking at his village, another vision came to him. He saw before him the figure of an old man. The old man was strangely familiar, even though Little One had never seen him before.

"Look upon me," the old man said. "What do you see?"

"I see an old man whose face is wrinkled with age," Little One said.

"Look upon me again," the old man said.

Then Little One looked, and as he looked, the lesson shown him by the willow tree filled his heart.

"I see an aged man in sacred clothing," Little One said. "The fluttering down of the eagle adorns his head. I see you, my grandfather. I see an aged man with the stem of the pipe between his lips. I see you, my grandfather. You are firm and rooted to the earth like the ancient willow. I see you standing among the days that are peaceful and beautiful. I see you, my grandfather. I see you standing as you will stand in your lodge, my grandfather."

The ancient man smiled. Little One had seen truly.

"My young brother," the old man said, "your mind is fixed upon the days that are peaceful and beautiful." And then he was gone.

Now Little One's heart was filled with peace, and as he walked into the village, his mind was troubled no longer with those questions about the meaning of life. For he knew that the old man he had seen was himself. The ancient man was Little One as he would be when he became an elder, filled with that great peace and wisdom which would give strength to all of the people. From that day on, Little One began to spend more time listening to the words his elders spoke, and of all the young men in the village, he was the happiest and the most content.

THE SOUTHWEST

The people of the Southwest live in one of the most var-ied and beautiful places on the continent. The dry desert areas and the high mountains and mesas of the lands of the Navajo, Pueblo, and Apache peoples con-trast with the seacoast and the river valleys that are home to the Yuki.

The Apache lived in the harsh deserts of what is now Arizona, moving seasonally to follow game and living in wickiups—portable dwellings that they covered with brush. Self-reliance was stressed as part of an Apache boy's coming to manhood. The Navajo, before the introduction of sheepherding, were much like their Apache cousins. They moved from one part of their ter-ritory to another and lived either in isolated hogans made of logs or in small family communities.

Both the Navajo and Apache gained a reputation for fierceness because of their defense of their homelands against those who sought to enslave or remove them.

That warrior tradition can be seen in such stories as the Apache tale "The Owl-Man Giant and the Monster Elk" and the Navajo story "How the Hero Twins Found Their Father."

The Pueblo story "The Bear Boy" is one that conveys a dual message. In a culture where people rely on one another and children are to be cherished, the neglectful father has as much to learn as the boy who wishes to become a man. And animals are seen not as mindless beings, but as wise creatures that can offer much knowledge to human beings who pay attention. In fact, the bear as a nurturing mother is a concept found almost everywhere in Native American culture. The turns of this particular story are ones that have always delighted me since I was first told the tale many years ago.

In California, things were not as hard as in the deserts of the Southwest. There, the Native people found that the climate was so mild and many kinds of food so plentiful, there was time for the development of complex family and community relationships. That complexity shows in their stories and rituals, as in the Yuki tale of one boy's initiation, "The Ghost Society."

The Owl-Man Giant
and the Monster Elk
Apache

Long ago, White-Painted Woman and her brother, Slayer of Enemies, lived on the earth. There were many monsters in those days, and one of the worst was Owl-Man Giant. Whenever Slayer of Enemies went hunting and shot a deer with his bow and arrows, Owl-Man Giant would come and take that deer. Owl-Man Giant was taller than the trees. He was hungry and fierce, and he wore a coat made of four layers of flint so that arrows could not kill him. Owl-Man Giant would come to the wickiup of White-Painted Woman and Slayer of Enemies and order them to give him food or he would eat them. White-Painted Woman prayed each morning that someone would help them.

One day, as she prayed, the Sun, who is the Giver of Life, came to her. "You are a brave woman," the Sun said, "so I wish you to be my wife."

White-Painted Woman agreed, and the two were married. But the Sun was not able to stay with her. His work was to bring light to all of the world.

"I must leave you," he said. "but you will have a child. He will be called Child of Water. You must hide him from the monsters. They know that he will destroy them when he is old enough."

Soon, White-Painted Woman gave birth to a boy. She named him Child of Water and hid him inside the wickiup in a hole under a basket in the corner. As soon as she hid him, Owl-Man Giant came to the door.

"I smell a child in there," the giant said. "I am hungry. Give him to me."

"There is no child in here," White-Painted Woman

said. And though Owl-Man Giant sniffed and searched, he could not find Child of Water. And so he went away.

One after another, each of the other monsters came to the wickiup seeking to eat the child, but White-Painted Woman kept him hidden and they went away.

"My son," White-Painted Woman said, "someday when you are grown, you will be very powerful. Then you will rid us of these monsters."

The boy grew quickly. One day he went to White-Painted Woman. "Mother," he said, "I am ready now to kill the monsters. Make a bow and arrows for me."

"First you must learn to hunt deer with your uncle, Slayer of Enemies," White-Painted Woman said. She made him a small wooden bow and arrows from the long grass.

Child of Water took the bow and arrows and followed his uncle. Slayer of Enemies led him along the canyons to the places where the deer could be found.

"Stay close to me," Slayer of Enemies said. "There are many monsters here in the canyons. Not only does Owl-Man Giant live nearby, there is also the Monster Elk. It is even bigger than Owl-Man Giant, and it tramples people before it eats them."

Child of Water listened carefully to his uncle and did as he was told. Soon they were able to creep close enough to a deer, and Child of Water shot his arrow. It struck the deer and killed it. But before they could reach the deer, Owl-Man Giant was there.

"This meat is mine," the giant said.

"My arrow killed the deer, so it is mine," said Child of Water. "You can have it only if you beat me in a contest."

"I agree," said Owl-Man Giant. "But I will set the

terms of this contest. Each of us will shoot four arrows at the other. You may go first."

"No," said Child of Water, "since I challenged you, it is right that I should allow you to go first."

Then Owl-Man Giant stepped back and picked up his bow, which was made from a huge tree. His four arrows were great logs with sharpened points. As he drew back his bow, lightning flashed all around them and a turquoise stone appeared at the feet of Child of Water.

"Pick me up," the turquoise stone said to the young man. "I will be your shield."

Child of Water looked to his uncle. Slayer of Enemies motioned for his nephew to pick up the stone. Child of Water held the turquoise stone before him. Owl-Man Giant fired his first arrow straight at the young man, but before it reached him, it rose up and went over Child of Water's head. Owl-Man Giant fired his second arrow, but before it reached the young man, it fell short. His third arrow went to the left, his fourth arrow to the right.

"Now," Child of Water said, "it is my turn."

Owl-Man Giant looked around for a stone that would protect him. He picked up a huge gray rock. Child of Water's first arrow split the rock and then knocked off the first coat of flint on the giant's armor. Owl-Man Giant picked up a bigger rock. But Child of Water's second arrow split that rock also and knocked away the next layer. Owl-Man Giant looked about for another rock but could not find one before Child of Water shot his third arrow, which removed the third layer from the giant's armor. Then, quickly, Child of Water fired his fourth arrow. It pierced the last coat of the giant's armor, went to his heart, and killed him.

Slayer of Enemies and Child of Water went back to their wickiup and told White-Painted Woman all that had happened.

"I do not believe it," White-Painted Woman said. "How can it be?"

When Child of Water showed his mother the pieces of flint from the giant's armor, she danced and sang with happiness.

"My son has come of age," she sang. "Now he will kill all the monsters that have troubled us for so long."

But Child of Water was not yet ready to dance and rejoice.

"Mother," he said, "I must go and kill the Monster Elk. It has been killing and eating the People for a long time."

Then Child of Water took his bow and arrows and set out. It was easy to find the trail of the Monster Elk. It was so huge and its hooves were so sharp that it left tracks in the stone. Some of those tracks can still be found in the stones to this day. Child of Water's plan was simple. He would shoot the great elk with his arrows. But when he stopped to sit down, he noticed that he had stepped close to a gopher hole and filled its entrance with dirt.

"Grandmother," Child of Water said, speaking to the gopher as an elder, "forgive me for blocking the door to your house." He leaned over and cleaned the dirt from the entrance to the gopher hole. When he had finished, the gopher stuck her head out of the hole.

"Grandson," said the gopher, "you have shown me great respect by clearing the doorway of my house and speaking to me as your grandmother. So I wish to warn you about the one you are hunting. The hair of the Monster Elk is so thick that even your arrows will not pierce it."

"What can I do?" said Child of Water. "This monster is eating the People. It will not be possible for human beings to live if I do not kill it."

"I will help you," the gopher said. "I know where the Monster Elk sleeps."

The gopher tunneled under the earth until she was beneath the place where the Monster Elk slept. She dug her hole right up to the monster's side, and she gnawed the hair away from the skin above its heart. There were four layers of hair, and the gopher had to work hard to remove all of them, but finally she was done. Then she went back underground to the place where Child of Water waited.

"There is only one spot where you can kill the horned monster," she said. "Shoot for the place over its heart where I chewed away all the hair."

"Grandmother," Child of Water said, "when I have killed the monster, you can be the first one to touch its body. That honor should be yours."

Then Child of Water continued on the trail until he was near the place where the monster slept. As soon as he was close enough, he shouted. The Monster Elk woke and jumped to its feet. Its horns were tall as trees. When it saw Child of Water, it bellowed so loudly that the ground shook. Child of Water drew back his arrow and let go. The arrow went straight to its target and struck the Monster Elk in its heart. The monster fell dead.

As soon as it fell, the gopher ran up to touch it. The

blood of the horned monster made her face and her paws dark. They are still dark to this day to remind people how she helped Child of Water.

When Child of Water came home, he called to his mother, "I have killed the Monster Elk."

"I do not believe it," said White-Painted Woman. "How can that be?"

Child of Water showed her the skin of the Monster Elk, and she rejoiced.

"My son," she said, "you have destroyed the monsters that have made this world unsafe for the People. The People to come will always remember you."

To this day, just as White-Painted Woman said, the Apache People remember Child of Water's great deeds, which made it safe for human beings to live on the earth. In honor of those deeds, they even made a special dance, to be danced whenever the People have to go to war. In it, the men play the part of Child of Water, and the women take the part of White-Painted Woman. It is a dance which reminds the People that when they go to fight, it should only be to protect the People from those who would destroy them.

How the Hero Twins
Found Their Father
Dine (Navajo)

One day long ago, Changing Woman was feeling lonely. She left her hogan and began to walk around. At last she came to a small waterfall. It was peaceful there, and she fell asleep with the sound of its water. As she slept, she dreamed that someone was there with her. When she woke, she saw footprints that had been burned into the stone. Those prints led to her from the east and went away from her to the west. So she realized that Sun had chosen her to be his wife.

In time she gave birth to two boys. She called them Older Twin and Younger Twin. Soon, however, the monsters who roamed the world in those days began to come to her hogan.

The giant Yeitso came to the hogan and loomed over it like a wall of stone. His skin was all covered with scales of flint, and he was taller than the hills. "Whose tracks are those around your hogan?" Yeitso rumbled. "They look like the tracks made by children at play."

"No," Changing Woman said, "I made those tracks myself with my hands. Because I am so lonely, I like to pretend that I have visitors."

That satisfied the giant and he went on his way. But other monsters continued to come and ask if there were children to be eaten. Finally, to discourage them and to keep her twin boys safe, Changing Woman grew cactus around the hogan. To this day, there is still cactus all over the lands where the Dine live.

As the boys grew up, they asked their mother one question again and again: "Who is our father?"

But she would never answer.

One day, when the boys were out together hunting for deer, Older Twin saw a tiny hole in the ground. Smoke was rising from it.

"Brother," he said, "look."

Younger Twin leaned over and touched the hole. As soon as he did so, a voice came from within.

"Grandchildren," it said, "come inside." Then the hole grew larger, and the twins went down into it on a ladder of thread that reached to the bottom. There, at the bottom of the hole, was an old lady. It was Spider Woman. She was the oldest of any beings on the earth, and those who respected her called her Grandmother. The walls of her cave were covered with beautiful feathers from all of the birds.

"Where are you going, grandchildren?" Spider Woman said.

"We are out hunting," Older Twin said.

"We want to find our father," said Younger Twin. "There are many monsters in the world, and they are troubling everyone. If we find our father, he may be able to help us destroy them."

"Your father is Johonaa'ei, the Sun," Spider Woman said. "I will help you find him."

Then Spider Woman gave each of the boys an eagle feather. "Keep these feathers," she said. "They will protect you. Now you must travel very far. Your journey will be hard, but my messenger Wind will go with you and show the way. First you must pass through Loka'aa Adigishii, the Cutting Reeds. If you remember the prayers I will teach you, you will pass through safely. But if you do not, the Cutting Reeds will kill you."

"Grandmother," Older Twin said, "we will remember what you tell us."

Grandmother Spider told them about the other dangers they would face on their way to the house of their father, the Sun. They would come to Seit'aad, Moving Sand. If they forgot their prayers and did not follow the right path, the sands would shift beneath them and then bury them. They would have to cross Nahodits'o, Swallowing Wash. It looked like the dry bed of a stream, but when people entered it, waters would rush in and they would drown. They would have to pass through Tse' Aheeninidil, Narrow Canyon, whose walls close in on travelers and crush them. In every place, if they took the wrong path or forgot to speak the right words, they would perish.

The twins were not afraid. Wind showed them the way, and they set out on their journey. Before long they came to the place where the reeds were sharp as obsidian knives. All around them they could see the bare bones of those who had tried to pass through and were killed by the reeds. Older Twin spoke the words they had been taught to the Cutting Reeds. "Loka'aa Adigishii," he said, speaking the powerful name of the Cutting Reeds, "allow us to pass."

The reeds were pleased to hear their name spoken. They parted, and holding tight to the eagle feathers, the twins passed through.

On they traveled until they came to Moving Sand. Now Younger Twin spoke to the sands.

"Moving Sand," he said, "allow us to pass."

The sands stopped shifting and the boys passed through. Wind showed them the way as they traveled, and soon they came to Swallowing Wash. This time Older Twin spoke.

"Swallowing Wash," he said, "allow us to pass." Then

the waters of Swallowing Wash became quiet and the boys passed through, following Wind, who showed them the way.

All went well until they came to Narrow Canyon. As they walked the trail into the canyon, both of the boys became afraid. The canyon walls started to close in on them, and they could not remember the right words to speak. But Wind blew on the eagle feathers and lifted them up high into the air. An eagle circled about them as they rose into the sky. The boys held on to their feathers and, flying with the eagle, they were carried to safety.

At last they came to the ocean. There two huge Water Striders waited for them. The twins greeted the Water Striders as Grandmother Spider had taught them.

"Talkaa Dijidii," the boys said, speaking the powerful names of the Water Striders, "we ask you to help us get to our father."

"We will carry you," said the Water Striders.

Older Twin and Younger Twin climbed on the backs of the insects, which carried them across the wide ocean to the land of Sun.

When they reached the house of the Sun, their father was not there. He had gone to travel all around the world as he did each day. Only a beautiful woman sat in Sun's hogan. She was the wife of Sun.

"Who are you?" she asked.

"We have come to see our father, Sun," Older Twin said.

"I believe your words are true, but my husband will not believe you," Sun's wife said. "Others have come here seeking power and claiming to be his children. He will try to kill you." Then she looked around the hogan.

On the east wall was a white curtain of cloud. On the south wall was a blue curtain of cloud. On the west wall was a yellow curtain, and on the north wall a black curtain of cloud. She reached out and pulled down the white cloud. "I will hide you from him," she said. She wrapped the boys in the white cloud so they could not be seen.

When Sun came home that night, the ground shook beneath his feet.

"Who has entered my hogan?" he asked.

But his wife would not answer him.

Sun began to look. He shook out each of the curtains. When he shook the last one, the white cloud on the east, the boys fell out on the floor.

"Father," Older Twin said, "we have come for you. We need your help to destroy the earth's monsters."

Sun did not believe the boys were his children.

"I must test you," he said. "If you are my sons, these knives will not kill you." Then he picked up the boys and threw them against the flint blades on the eastern side of his hogan. But the two boys held tight to their eagle feathers and flew above the blades.

"If you are my children," Sun said, "you can sleep in the ocean without freezing." Then he put the boys in the cold water and left them. Wind called to his friend the beaver, who came and warmed the boys so they did not freeze. When Sun came for them, they were alive and well. But he still did not believe them.

"I will make a sweat bath for you," Sun said. He called to his daughter and asked her to prepare a sweat house. The daughter did as Sun said. However, she had watched the boys pass the tests Sun gave them. She believed that the boys were his children, and decided to help them. When she made the sweat house, she dug a small hole at the back and covered it with a sheet of darkness and white shells.

"This is no ordinary sweat house," she whispered to the boys. "The lodge will be so hot that you will be killed. Climb into the pit in the back. You will be safe there."

As soon as the stones for the sweat bath were red-hot, Sun placed the boys in the lodge and covered it. The boys climbed into the pit in the back.

"Are you hot?" Sun asked.

"No," both boys answered.

Four times he asked, and four times they said no. Then Sun began to pour water on the hot stones in the middle of the lodge. The whole sweat house filled with scalding-hot steam. It was so hot that no human being could survive.

Sun waited a time before he spoke again. "Are you hot now?" he asked.

"Yes," both boys answered, "but the heat is pleasant."

At last Sun began to suspect that the boys were his children. But he prepared one more test. He filled a pipe with tobacco so strong that it would kill a normal person.

"We will smoke together," Sun said.

The boys agreed. Four times the pipe was passed around, but the boys held on to their eagle feathers, and the tobacco did not harm them. Now Sun knew they were indeed his sons.

"My daughter," he said, "prepare a bath for my sons." Then Older Twin and Younger Twin were bathed four times, first in a basket made of white beads, then in a basket made of turquoise, next in a basket made of white shells, and last in a basket made of black obsidian. Finally they were given new clothing.

"My sons," Johonaa'ei, the Sun, said, "I will give you the things you need to destroy the monsters." He reached up and took down two bows and two quivers of arrows from above his door. "These arrows are powerful weapons. They are the lightning that strikes crooked and the lightning that strikes straight. If I give them to you, you will surely kill the monsters. But when you have succeeded, you must return these bows and arrows."

"Thank you, Father," the twins said as they accepted the weapons.

"I must now give you new names," Sun said. "You who are older, your name is Monster Slayer. You who are younger, your name is now Born of Water because it was near the waterfall that I met your mother."

Then Sun dressed them in armor made of flint and lowered the two boys down to earth on a bolt of lightning.

When they stepped off the bolt, they were on top of Tsoodzil, Mount Taylor. As they walked down the south side of the mountain, they came to a high wall of stones.

"Brother," said Born of Water, "let us try our weapons and see how strong they are."

"That is good," said Monster Slayer.

So they shot their arrows. The lightning that strikes straight and the lightning that strikes crooked shattered the cliff, making a big cleft in it.

"We will do well with these weapons," Born of Water said.

As they walked down the mountain, they heard a rumbling like the sound of an earthquake. It was the giant Yeitso, who had smelled their scent and was coming to look for them, walking in a great circle around the hills. First they saw the top of his head over the hills to the east; then they saw his head and shoulders over the hills to the south. The ground shook even harder; and they saw the whole upper half of his body over the hills to the west. Finally the giant stood before them, just on the other side of Blue Water Lake. He bent over and drank until the lake was almost empty.

Born of Water and Monster Slayer stood upon a bent rainbow, and their reflections showed in the remaining water of the lake.

"What are these handsome little things?" Yeitso growled. "Why have I not seen them before, and how shall I kill them?"

Wind came to the shoulders of the twins and whispered to them. "Throw his words back to him."

"What is this big thing and why have we never seen him before?" the twins said. "How shall we kill him?"

Yeitso roared and fired an arrow at the boys. The bent rainbow on which the boys stood straightened, and the arrow passed over their heads. Yeitso fired a second bolt and the rainbow arced again. This time the giant's arrow passed beneath their feet. The giant's third arrow went to their left, his fourth to their right.

Then Born of Water shot his arrow. The lightning that strikes crooked hit Yeitso and knocked him back. Monster Slayer shot his arrow, and the lightning that strikes straight knocked Yeitso down and killed him. His flint scales shattered from his body and scattered all over the land.

"That flint will be useful to our people in the future,"

Monster Slayer said. Then the two brothers cut off the giant's head to make sure he would not come back to life again. As soon as they did so, Yeitso's blood began to flow down the valley.

"If his blood goes far enough, Yeitso will return to life," Wind whispered to the brothers. Quickly Monster Slayer cut a line in the rock and stopped the flow. Yeitso's blood dried and it remains there to this day, though the newcomers call it beds of lava.

Monster Slayer and Born of Water went home to Changing Woman. She did not believe what she was told until they showed her Yeitso's broken arrows, which they had brought with them. Soon the two brothers set forth again to slay the other monsters. They killed the One Who Kicks People Off the Cliffs; they killed the Monster Bird, the Eyes That Slay, the Bear That Pursues, and the Rolling Rock. Then they made a huge storm sweep across the land in the place where the monsters hid. When the storm ended, a great canyon existed where the many terrible creatures had once been. Today it is called the Grand Canyon by the newcomers.

"Now," Monster Slayer said, "we have killed all of the monsters that threatened the People."

But Wind came and whispered in Monster Slayer's ear, "Four still remain to bring death and trouble to the People."

So Monster Slayer and Born of Water set out to finish the work they had begun. They traveled in the direction Wind told them to go, toward the north. At last they found a cavern and went inside. This was the place where they would find the last ones that would trouble the Dine.

"Here is one of them," Born of Water said, standing

over an old man who crouched in a corner with an empty bowl. "It is Dichin." And indeed it was so. The old man was Dichin, whose name means "Hunger."

"I will kill you," said Monster Slayer. "Then the People will never again feel the pain of hunger."

"Do not kill me," said the old man. "It is hunger that makes food enjoyable. Without hunger the People would have no reason to go out and hunt for their food."

"This is true," said Monster Slayer. "We will spare you."

"Here," cried Born of Water, indicating an old woman wrapped in a blanket. "Here is one to slay. This is Hakaz Estan, Cold Woman."

Monster Slayer lifted up his hand. "Then she must die. No longer will the People shiver from the cold."

"No," said Cold Woman, "I am needed. Without me, the springs will dry up. The land will be too hot and the People will not survive."

"You are right," Monster Slayer said. "We must spare you also."

"This one here," Born of Water cried. "This one here with the ragged clothing is Tgaei. Surely it is right that we should destroy Poverty."

But Tgaei spoke up as the others had. "Without me, old things will never wear out. It will not be well for the People in the days to come if there is no poverty. Old things must wear out for there to be new ones."

"Then we shall spare you as well," Monster Slayer said.

"Brother," said Born of Water, "this old, old woman leaning on her stick is Sa. Old Age must be killed so that the People will not have to grow old and die."

But Old Age held up her hand. "No," Sa said, "you

must not destroy me. Without old age, people will not appreciate their lives. Let there be old age so that new people will have space to come into the world."

Again Monster Slayer and Born of Water had to agree. And so it is that hunger and cold, poverty and old age remain with us to this day.

Then Monster Slayer and Born of Water returned to their father, the Sun. They gave back their borrowed weapons, for the twins had done their work. But they were told that if they needed those weapons once more to save the People from monsters, they would be welcome in the house of their father to receive his help.

So it happened long ago, but the People say that the Hero Twins still have their dwelling in the valley of the San Juan River. Sometimes, when Dine men go to war, they go to that valley to pray for help from the Hero Twins. And if those old monsters—or new ones—come to threaten the lives of the People, the Dine know that the Hero Twins will visit the house of their father again.

The Bear Boy
Pueblo

Long ago, in a Pueblo village, a boy named Kuo-Haya lived with his father. But his father did not treat him well. In his heart he still mourned the death of his wife, Kuo-Haya's mother, and did not enjoy doing things with his son. He did not teach his boy how to run. He did not show him how to wrestle. He was always too busy.

As a result, Kuo-Haya was a timid boy and walked about stooped over all of the time. When the other boys raced or wrestled, Kuo-Haya slipped away. He spent much of his time alone.

Time passed, and the boy reached the age when his father should have been helping him get ready for his initiation into manhood. Still Kuo-Haya's father paid no attention at all to his son.

One day Kuo-Haya was out walking far from the village, toward the cliffs where the bears lived. Now the people of the village always knew they must stay away from these cliffs, for the bear was a very powerful animal. It was said that if someone saw a bear's tracks and followed them, he might never come back. But Kuo-Haya had never been told about this. When he came upon the tracks of a bear, Kuo-Haya followed them along an arroyo, a small canyon cut by a winding stream, up into the mesas. The tracks led into a little box canyon below some caves. There, he came upon some bear cubs.

When they saw Kuo-Haya, the little bears ran away. But Kuo-Haya sat down and called to them in a friendly voice.

"I will not hurt you," he said to the bear cubs. "Come and play with me."

The bears walked back out of the bushes. Soon the boy and the bears were playing together. As they played, however, a shadow came over them. Kuo-Haya looked up and saw the mother bear standing above him.

"Where is Kuo-Haya?" the people asked his father.

"I do not know," the father said.

"Then you must find him!"

So the father and the other people of the pueblo began to search for the missing boy. They went through the canyons calling his name. But they found no sign of the boy there. Finally, when they reached the cliffs, the best trackers found his footsteps and the path of the bears. They followed the tracks along the arroyo and up into the mesas to the box canyon. In front of a cave, they saw the boy playing with the bear cubs as the mother bear watched them approvingly, nudging Kuo-Haya now and then to encourage him.

The trackers crept close, hoping to grab the boy and run. But as soon as the mother bear caught their scent, she growled and pushed her cubs and the boy back into the cave.

"The boy is with the bears," the trackers said when they returned to the village.

"What shall we do?" the people asked.

"It is the responsibility of the boy's father," said the medicine man. Then he called Kuo-Haya's father to him.

"You have not done well," said the medicine man. "You are the one who must guide your boy to manhood, but you have neglected him. Now the mother bear is caring for your boy as you should have done all along. She is teaching him to be strong as a young man must be strong. If you love your son, only you can get him back."

Every one of the medicine man's words went into the father's heart like an arrow. He began to realize that he had been blind to his son's needs because of his own sorrow.

"You are right," he said. "I will go and bring back my son."

Kuo-Haya's father went along the arroyo and climbed the cliffs. When came to the bears' cave, he found Kuo-Haya wrestling with the little bears. As the father watched, he saw that his son seemed more sure of himself than ever before.

"Kuo-Haya," he shouted. "Come to me."

The boy looked at him and then just walked into the cave. Although the father tried to follow, the big mother bear stood up on her hind legs and growled. She would not allow the father to come any closer.

So Kuo-Haya's father went back to his home. He was angry now. He began to gather together his weapons, and brought out his bow and his arrows and his lance. But the medicine man came to his lodge and showed him the bear claw that he wore around his neck.

"Those bears are my relatives!" the medicine man said. "You must not harm them. They are teaching your boy how we should care for each other, so you must not be cruel to them. You must get your son back with love, not violence."

Kuo-Haya's father prayed for guidance. He went outside and sat on the ground. As he sat there, a bee flew up to him, right by his face. Then it flew away. The father stood up. Now he knew what to do!

"Thank you, Little Brother," he said. He began to make his preparations. The medicine man watched what he was doing and smiled.

Kuo-Haya's father went to the place where the bees had their hives. He made a fire and put green branches on it so that it made smoke. Then he blew the smoke into the tree where the bees were. The bees soon went to sleep.

Carefully Kuo-Haya's father took out some honey from their hive. When he was done, he placed pollen and some small pieces of turquoise at the foot of the tree to thank the bees for their gift. The medicine man, who was watching all this, smiled again. Truly the father was beginning to learn.

Kuo-Haya's father traveled again to the cliffs where the bears lived. He hid behind a tree and saw how the mother bear treated Kuo-Haya and the cubs with love. He saw that Kuo-Haya was able to hold his own as he wrestled with the bears.

He came out from his hiding place, put the honey on the ground, and stepped back. "My friends," he said, "I have brought you something sweet."

The mother bear and her cubs came over and began to eat the honey. While they ate, Kuo-Haya's father went to the boy. He saw that his little boy was now a young man.

"Kuo-Haya," he said, putting his hands on his son's shoulders, "I have come to take you home. The bears have taught me a lesson. I shall treat you as a father should treat his son."

"I will go with you, Father," said the boy. "But I, too, have learned things from the bears. They have shown me how we must care for one another. I will come with you only if you promise you will always be friends with the bears."

The father promised, and that promise was kept. Not only was he friends with the bears, but he showed his boy the love a son deserves. And he taught him all the things a son should be taught.

Everyone in the village soon saw that Kuo-Haya, the bear boy, was no longer the timid little boy he had been. Because of what the bears had taught him, he was the best wrestler among the boys. With his father's help, Kuo-Haya quickly became the greatest runner of all. To this day, his story is told to remind all parents that they must always show as much love for their children as there is in the heart of a bear.

The Ghost Society
Yuki

It was not yet morning, but Walks Slow could not sleep. If he was right, as soon as the morning light arrived, the men would enter the *han* and take him. They would spend the day making him ready, and then in the evening they would go to the *iwl-han*, the dance house. There Walks Slow—if he was one of the boys chosen this time—would be initiated into the Hulk'ilal-woknam, the Ghost Society. To belong to the Ghost Society meant that a boy was no longer a little child. He was one who had been taught the things that were needed to become a man. Still, the thought of having to face the powerful beings who came to do that initiation, beings who looked something like the older men of his village but who were actually powerful ghost spirits, worried Walks Slow.

This will happen, he thought. It was the right time of year, the season known as the Moon When Acorns Get Ready to Drop. He had seen the signs that preparations were taking place for the ceremony, even though no one spoke openly about it. It had been three winters since the last Hulk'ilal-woknam. And there was one every fourth year. Walks Slow was sure he would be chosen. He was old enough. He had seen three handfuls of winters. He was one of the boys who was praised for his ability to do things that helped the people. He was strong, a good hunter, a good runner. After the Hulk'ilal-woknam, he would be even stronger, even better at running and hunting. Surely he would be chosen.

Walks Slow had been through the Taikomol initiation three winters ago. They had taken him with the other children to the dance house early in the morning, and he had sat straight without moving from dawn till the middle of the day, hearing the old man with his cocoon rattle and eagle feather tell them the stories of creation that all true Yuki must know. Shum-hohtme, "Big Ear," was the old man's name, and he was a powerful man. His tellings of the ancient tales made them come alive in the darkened dance house.

Walks Slow's mother and father were behind him throughout the whole initiation, ready to prop him up if he wavered from his cross-legged stance or fell back as children sometimes did. But he sat straight and listened, taking into his memory every word.

Although he had done well then, he was still worried. He lay near the back of the house with his head close to the center post of their *han*, looking up at the roof overhead, the interlaced poles that were well covered with bark. The light flickered from the firepit, and a few sparks rose up like new stars going into the sky. He could see the entrance tunnel into their house, the woven basket door still closed. Soon it would be pushed aside and the men would enter. His hands were trembling. Walks Slow tried to calm his mind by thinking of the story old Shum-hohtme had told of how it all began, how the world was made, how the Taikomol-woknam came to be.

Even Taikomol, "He Who Walks Alone," made mistakes. It was from the north that Taikomol came. There was only water, no land, and Taikomol made land upon it. He built the first *iwl-han* on that land. He made human beings from sticks. But he had done this too quickly. The land sank, and the dance house and the first people sank with it. Again Taikomol was alone, with nothing but water around him.

So Taikomol created another world. There was no sun yet and no daylight and Taikomol had made no game animals to eat. In the darkness, the people hunted and ate one another. Things did not go right in that world. Fire came into it and burned everything up, even the water.

At last Taikomol made one more world. This time he started from the north and then extended it to the southeast. He made the sun, and daylight shone on the land. The land was new, white, and clean. He walked to the south, and as he walked, he saw the land stretching farther than he could see. But the land was not yet finished. Taikomol made rivers flow and mountains rise up. Then he built another dance house. The world swayed like a log floating in the water. The ground was not firm beneath it. Taikomol made a great elk, a great deer, a great coyote. He placed them in the north of the new land, but the land continued to move.

"Lie down and hold this earth firm," he said. They did so, and the land stopped swaying. As long as they lie still, the land is firm, but whenever one of them forgets and stands up again, the earth shakes. To this day, when earthquakes come, the people say it is because those animals are not lying still.

Then Taikomol went into his dance house. He placed sticks on the floor. "You will wake up as human beings and have a feast," Taikomol said. Then he went outside and stood at the door of the dance house. He waited all night. When it was morning, the sound of many voices talking came from inside the dance house. At last the first human beings emerged.

That was how it began, Walks Slow thought, with the new day. It seemed as if he could see the faintest glimmer of light from around the edges of the basket door. Suddenly the basket was snatched away from the door, and men came into the house. They grabbed him by the arms and feet and threw him out the door. In the early light of the new day, Walks Slow could see a few other boys outside. The men guided them from one house to another and then led them out of the village to the next settlement. By the end of the day, they had gathered boys from the camps all around. The twenty-four boys had been led through the woods. And now, as evening came, they were placed in front of the new *iwl-han* that had been built for this special occasion.

Walks Slow sat close to the door of the new dance house. He had been one of the first boys taken that morning and he had eaten nothing all day, but he was not hungry. Excitement filled his stomach. He was waiting for the drum. He knew it would be coming, for a handful of days ago, he had found the place where the men were building that drum. He had smelled the smoke and followed it through the hills until he heard the singing and looked down through the bushes to the place where the men were hollowing out the log. *"Helegadadie hiye, helegadadie hiye"* came the drum-beat song.

Then, from the dusk to the north of the dance house, he heard it coming. As the men carried the log, now painted the black that showed it to be a true drum, they sang that song, *"Helegadadie hiye."* As they reached the entrance, they swung the end of the drum in through the wood hole and then swung it out. Again and again they swung the drum, until on the fourth sacred time they actually brought it into the dance house. Soon, Walks Slow could hear the sound of the men's feet dancing on the drum, and he knew it was in its place over the ditch in the back of the house.

As the drum became silent, figures came out of the darkness and picked up Walks Slow, carrying him toward the door. They swung him four times and then released him to be caught by other hands inside. He blinked his eyes as he was seated, but he could see nothing. He could sense people standing about him and knew they must be the Hulk'ilal, the Ghosts.

Walks Slow trembled at the thought of their presence, recalling how Taikomol had put together the first Hulk'ilal-woknam. He asked his friend and helper Coyote to arrange the first ceremony, but Coyote did it wrong. Instead of having people wear costumes and play the part of the ghosts, Coyote brought in real ghosts. As a result, all of the people watching the ceremony or taking part in it died. Taikomol had to make new people. This time he arranged the ceremony himself instead of letting Coyote do it.

Walks Slow felt people moving about him in the dark. Then everything was still. All of the boys were now in their places in the dance house. Suddenly the fire burst up in the center of the house as the drum began to sound and the singing of "*Helina heluli, helina heluli, helina heluli, helina heluli*" began. Soon another noise split the air—the sound of men shaking their throats with their fingers as they shouted:

YUWWUWUWUWUW

Walks Slow wanted to jump up and run, but he could not. The ghosts were all around him and the other boys. They looked much like certain older men he knew well. But they were painted black and white in broad horizontal stripes. Their hair was not like human hair—it was as thick and stringy as maple bark. Their heads were circled by a wreath of black oak and manzanita leaves, their faces puffed out as a man's face would be if he stuffed his cheeks with grass. Something like a long, springy twig grew from the center of each Hulk'ilal's face, bent from the nostrils to the lower lip.

A human voice came from near the drum, speaking to the ghosts. "Where do you come from? Why are you here, saying nothing?"

Then the leaders of the ghosts hopped forward, twisting their arms back and forth. "We have come to see how you do this. We were sent by the One above. We came to see this fire, this drum, and the other things you are doing. We will not be here long."

Food was brought out, and it was given to the boys as they sat. Some, like Walks Slow, tried to refuse the food, but an older man who Walks Slow recognized as his mother's brother bent low and said to him, "This is the last food you will have for four days. Eat it while you can."

The Hulk'ilal then began to dance on the drum. One after another, each ghost leaped on the drum four times.

"Heye," shouted each ghost as he jumped.

"Yoho, yoho," the men in the dance house answered back.

The fire was built up even more, and it grew hotter. Everyone's body and face were beaded with sweat. All through the night the Hulk'ilal danced, and Walks Slow found himself not knowing if he was awake or asleep. It was a dance that would bring the people plenty to eat in the years to come. There would be deer and acorns and all other foods. At times more older men came into the house, and the dance-house leader greeted them, shaking his cocoon rattle. One of the old men was the father of Walks Slow's father.

A dance began and the boys were made to join in, and Walks Slow's grandfather danced behind him, keeping him close to the fire as they circled it, so that he would sweat even more. The dance leader grabbed a burning log from the fire and went about the circle, blowing sparks from it onto the boys.

"Yu'u, yu'u," Walks Slow's grandfather whispered in his ear.

Some shrank back, but Walks Slow held out his arms, crying the courage sounds his grandfather had reminded him of, "Yu'u, yu'u," even as the sparks landed on his wrists and forearms.

So it went on through that night and into the next day. They danced and sweated and sat and listened to the words and songs inside the dance house. Soon, there was no longer any awareness of day or night, or of any world other than that inside the dance house.

At last it was noon on the fourth day. Walks Slow and the other boys lay back as they had been told, their eyes closed, holding their breath as if they were dead. They were about to be born again. Walks Slow felt himself being lifted up, carried, and swung back and forth again and again and again. Suddenly he went flying through the air. He felt as if he were floating, as Taikomol must have floated before there was earth on which to walk. Then hands and arms caught him, and he opened his eyes. His parents and his grandfather and his aunt and uncle were holding him. They had caught him, just as the other boys were now being caught by their relatives as they were thrown out through the door of the dance house. The unfamiliar light of day made Walks Slow blink his eyes, but he laughed and his relatives laughed with him. He had been thrown out into manhood.

THE NORTHWEST

The stories that represent rite-of-passage experiences from the northwestern part of the American continent include tales from the buffalo-hunting peoples of the plains, the Cheyenne and Lakota, who maintained a chivalric code of honor in their lives as hunters and warriors; the people of the northern Pacific coast, where the lives and the stories of the people always focused on the sea; and the people of the northern coast of Alaska, where one of the most unforgiving climates in the world has bred a people who have learned every way to find the edge that will ensure their survival.

There are some elements in the stories from the plains that will be familiar by now. There is the vision quest in "The Light-haired Boy," the true story of a strange Lakota boy who wished to help his people by gaining power through fasting. In the Cheyenne tale "Star Boy," there is a mythic hero who has inherited power from his father, a sky-being, and uses it to kill the monsters that threaten his human relatives.

The two stories from the far Northwest and the far-thest north have some different events in them. In the Tlingit tale "Salmon Boy," the hero not only goes down to an underwater world, as the chief's son does in the Creek story of the tie-snakes, but he is actually trans-formed into a salmon himself. This story teaches respect for the fish that are the source of life for his peo-ple, and it also makes clear how close the worlds of humans and nonhumans are in the eyes of the Tlingit.

The true story "Tommy's Whale" was told to me seven years ago in Alaska by the man who was that boy (though his name has been changed in my telling). It may require some further introduction, especially since it is about the hunting of a great member of an endangered species. As I hope this story makes clear, the Inupiaq have great respect and even love for the whale. As the Inupiaq poet Fred Bigjim puts it, "Bow-head whale, you give us our culture."

At one time, the bowhead whale was almost wiped out, but it was not the Inupiaq who did that killing. They never took more than they needed to live. Now the number of bowhead has increased significantly. Thousands of whales again swim beneath the ice of the Bering Sea.

A few years ago, it was agreed by the International Whaling Congress, in close consultation with the Inupiaq Whaling Association, that the Inupiaq could hunt the bowhead whale again, but only under the strictest of controls. Each of a few villages is allowed to strike no more than three whales each year. As my friend who allowed me to tell his story said, "Even now, though we hunt the great whale, we do so with respect. We love the whale, and in return for our love it gives itself to us."

The Light-haired Boy
Lakota

It was the year 1841 and the time of the Moon of Falling Leaves. There, in the heart of the Paha Sapa, the sacred Black Hills, a boy was born. His father was Tashunka Witco, a holy man of the Oglala, one of the bands of the Lakota Nation. His mother was a member of the Brule Nation. Because this boy's hair was sandy brown, lighter, thinner, and curlier than any other Lakota boy's, he was soon given the nickname Curly.

As the seasons passed, the light-haired boy named Curly grew, but he did not grow as quickly as the other boys his age. He was strong and wiry, but he would never be tall. His hair and skin remained lighter than those of the other boys. They were so light that some of the Wasichu, those pale new people who liked to take the best of everything, sometimes thought he was one of them, a white boy who had been taken captive and adopted.

By the time Curly reached his thirteenth year, no one questioned that he was a real Lakota. He had killed a buffalo from horseback with his bow and arrows. He had been the first to ride a wild horse caught by his father. In fact, since he had ridden and been given that horse, his father and his father's best friend, a warrior named High Backbone, had a different name for the boy. They called him His Horse On Sight. But Curly was still the name spoken most often in camp.

Around the time Curly first learned to ride the wild horse, a meeting was held that would change the lives of many Lakota forever. It was August of 1854, in the Moon of Wild Plums. There was trouble between the Wasichu and the Lakota. A cow belonging to a settler had wandered into a Lakota camp circle. When it ran into his teepee, a man named High Forehead shot that cow. Then he butchered it and shared it with the people. After all, the promised government food rations were long overdue. It was only fair they should eat a cow that had volunteered itself in this way.

The matter should have been easy to solve, for though they joked about it, the Lakota were ready to pay for the cow. But that was not enough for the young warrior chief at the fort. He demanded of the Minneconjou band that Conquering Bear, one of the twenty-four chiefs of the Lakota Nation, meet with the white soldiers who were coming to the chief's village. And Conquering Bear must have High Forehead ready—to be handed over for punishment.

Conquering Bear agreed to the meeting. When the soldiers arrived at the Minneconjou village, not far from the Oglala camp where Curly lived, they were heavily armed. They were led by Lieutenant John H. Gratton. "Give me a handful of men and three cannons," Gratton had once said, "and I'll defeat the whole Sioux nation." Seeing this man at the head of the soldiers worried Conquering Bear even more, for they had brought the big guns carried in wagons. He had asked that no wagon guns be brought. Without wagon guns, they might be able to parley peacefully. Gratton, however, was spoiling for a fight. He ordered his thirty troopers to aim their carbines and the cannons at the lodge of Conquering Bear, where the chief stood with his other chiefs about him.

To make matters even worse, the Wasichu's interpreter, Wyuse, was known to be a man who spoke the truth only when it would benefit him.

"Minneconjou," Wyuse said, "you are dogs. You are cowards, men afraid to fight."

Then Lieutenant Gratton began to speak. His words were angry. It was possible that Wyuse interpreted them truthfully to Conquering Bear. But Conquering Bear's words were twisted like aspen leaves in the wind.

"We will give you five good horses for that one cow," Conquering Bear said in Lakota.

"The chief will not give you anything," Wyuse said in English.

"We do not wish to fight. We only want peace," Conquering Bear pleaded in Lakota.

"The chief says you are all afraid to shoot," Wyuse said in English, sneering.

As Wyuse spoke those words, Gratton barked an order. The thirty troopers fired a salvo. The men must have been nervous, for most of them failed to hit anything. But Conquering Bear's brother, who stood beside the chief, was struck in the chest by a bullet. Blood came from his mouth and he fell to the ground.

Some of the Lakota began to run. Conquering Bear stood his ground and held up his empty hands.

"Do not fight," he shouted to his people. "Now that the Wasichu have shot a good man, they will go away."

Even as Conquering Bear spoke, Gratton ordered another volley. The soldiers fired again, and three bullets struck Conquering Bear. He fell beside his brother. It seemed as if the Wasichu soldiers meant to wipe out the whole village. High Forehead grabbed a rifle and fired. His bullet hit and killed Lieutenant Gratton. Then the Lakota began to fight in earnest. Spotted Tail, another Lakota chief and the brother of Curly's mother, had been waiting with a group of his own men in a nearby ravine, in case of trouble. At the sound of the shots, they came running. Arrows rained down on the thirty soldiers. When it was over, all of the Wasichu were wiped out. So, too, was Wyuse, whose crooked words had made the trouble worse. His Lakota brother-in-law pierced the interpreter's ears with a lance. "Now," he said, "your ears are open. Next time they will not be closed when we speak to you."

That day, Curly was in the Minneconjou camp. From the other side, where he and a group of boys had been told to wait, he heard the shots and came running. The battle was over by the time he arrived. He helped other Lakota men and boys to overturn the wagon guns, pile brush over them, and set them on fire. Then he helped the Minneconjou break camp, and rode back to his own Oglala camp to help his own people do the same. They would move far away from the fort, for more trouble would surely follow this. Curly had learned a lesson that day. Never again would he trust the Wasichu soldiers. How could anyone trust people who would come into a peaceful camp and shoot a man in front of his own lodge?

For a few days it seemed as if the Lakota would have to go to war, but people on both sides spoke for peace. Among them was Conquering Bear, gravely wounded but not dead. The talk of war began to die down, and the soldiers at the fort did not retaliate. Gratton's actions had been provocative and war with the Lakota at this time was something no one wanted. The Oglala and Minneconjou moved even deeper into the Black Hills, away from the Laramie River and the fort. There, in the heart of the Paha Sapa, wrapped in his robes, Conquering Bear waited for his death.

High Backbone was one of Conquering Bear's most devoted warriors and kept vigil at the side of his dying chief. Because of High Backbone, Curly was allowed into the lodge of Conquering Bear. The sight of that gentle old man's drawn yellow face deeply affected the boy. He took his horse and rode away from the camp, knowing what he had to do. He rode along the bluffs above the river till he came to an eagle-catching pit dug into the soft earth. It was in such holes, concealed by branches placed on top with a freshly killed rabbit laid out for bait, that a man would wait for an eagle to land. Then he would grab the bird by its legs so that he could take some of its powerful feathers.

Curly tied his hobbling rope between the legs of his pinto so it would not wander far as it grazed at the bottom of the hill. The horse was close to a stream and could drink. He climbed the hill, stripped off all his clothes except for a breechclout, and stepped down into the uncovered pit. He sat back on the cold gravel, looked up at the sky, and prayed for a vision.

The first day passed and the night came. Curly did not leave the eagle-catching pit. He continued to pray for a vision, for strength to help his people in this hard time. The seasons to come would be even harder for the Lakota. He needed a vision to help them. But the second day passed, and the second night, and no vision came. Without food or water, Curly continued to cry for a vision.

"Wakan Tanka," he called, "Great Mystery, I am small and pitiful. I want to help my people."

It was a strange thing that the boy was doing on that hilltop. To fast and pray for a vision was not strange in itself. But *hanblecheyapi,* "crying for a vision," was one of the seven sacred rites of the Lakota people, and it was always supposed to be done in the right way. He had not done a purifying sweat to prepare himself. His elders had not prepared him for his vigil. His father had not taken him to the hilltop and showed him where to wait. But Curly continued with his strange vision quest, even after the dawn of the third day brought nothing to his eyes or ears. No spirit, no bird or animal, not even an insect came to him. All that he saw was the sky above and the earth and stones of the eagle-catching pit.

At last, late in the afternoon of that third day, Curly climbed out of the eagle-catching pit. After going so long without food or drink, he was barely able to stand. It seemed no vision would ever come to him, and he wondered if he was not worthy. He felt weak and sick as he made his way slowly down the hill to the place where his pinto grazed near a cottonwood tree. When he reached that tree, he could stand no longer. He slumped down against the tree and leaned his back against it.

And then the rider came. The rider came toward him on the back of Curly's own pinto, yet the horse and the man were floating in the air as they rode. They were more in the spirit world than in this world where Curly sat leaning against a tree. Suddenly the pinto changed. It became a bay horse, and then a spotted one. The man was closer now, and Curly saw that he wore blue leggings and had no paint on his face. His hair was long and brown, and a single feather hung from it. Behind one ear, a round stone was tied. A red-tailed hawk flew above the man's head. Then Curly heard words that were not spoken. They came to him from that warrior, telling him the day would come when he would dress that way. He would never wear a headdress or tie up his horse's tail, but he would be among the bravest of the brave.

The air became filled with the streaking of hail and bullets. Yet nothing touched that rider as he continued on. Storm clouds rolled above him and the thunder sounded, but the man continued to ride. Now there was a mark on the man's cheek like a lightning bolt, and spots on his chest like the marks of hail. Curly knew that he would paint himself that way one day when he rode to fight for his people. Then, as the man rode, there were people all around him, other Lakota. Some of them reached up to hold the rider back or pull him from his horse.

Curly felt hands on his shoulders, shaking him. He opened his eyes. His own father, Tashunka Witco, and his warrior uncle, High Backbone, were bending over him, concern in their faces. Curly looked past them and saw his pinto still grazing peacefully, hobbled as it had been before his vision began. No rider was on its back, but in the top of the bush next to the horse, a red-tailed hawk perched and called four times.

"Why are you here?" his father asked.

"It is not safe to ride off alone," High Backbone said. "There are raiding parties out, and the Wasichu may still make war on us."

"I came to seek a vision," Curly said. He wanted to tell the men what he had seen so they could help him better understand it. His father was a holy man and would surely know what it meant. But his father's face filled with anger.

"You were not prepared for *hanblecheyapi*," Tashunka Witco said. "How could you come out to fast without going first into the *inipi*, the sweat lodge? How can you expect a true vision without being guided by your elders?"

Curly looked over at High Backbone. He, too, was angry. They would not listen to him, so he said nothing. He did not speak of his vision. He let them carry him back to the camp, where he drank the soup given to him and then slept. When he woke, he still did not speak. He kept his vision in his heart but shared it with no one. Three winters passed, and his vision remained unshared.

Throughout those years, Tashunka Witco and High Backbone kept their eyes on the boy. They saw clearly that he had been changed for the better by whatever had come to him on that hill, but they did not ask him to tell of it.

Then, in the summer of 1857, during the Moon of Wild Plums, there was a great gathering of all the many camps of the Lakota Nation. Never before had Curly seen so many of his people together. All the Oglala, the Brule, the Minneconjou, the Sans Arc, the Blackfoot Lakota, the Two Kettles, and the Hunkpapa—the seven great camp circles—were there. They met in the valley below Bear Butte, in the heart of the Paha Sapa. Curly's heart was filled with love and pride for his people. And Tashunka Witco looked into his son's heart and saw that it was time for them to speak of what Curly had seen on his lonely vision quest.

The father and son rode off into the hills until they came to the valley near Rapid Creek on the eastern side of the Paha Sapa, where Curly had been born. Tashunka Witco constructed a sweat lodge and purified his son and himself. Then Curly began to talk. His father listened as he told of the powerful vision given to him.

Tashunka Witco was silent for a long time after his son finished. He looked into the fire and then spoke himself. "The man on that horse is the one you will become. You will dress and paint yourself as he did. You must always be first in fighting for our people, even though they will try to hold you back. And because of that vision, you must have a new name. I will give you my own name, and from now on, it will be yours to carry. From now on, you will be Tashunka Witco."

The young man whose name had been Curly listened to his father's words. He understood why his father had given him his name, for it fit his vision of a horse dancing through a storm. From that day on, he would be known by that name, and his name would come to stand for the bravest of all the Lakota. He would become a warrior who would never be touched by a bullet in battle, even though he was always in the front of every fight. He would be one of the principal leaders of the Lakota in the great battle at the Little Big Horn, where his people would defeat the Seventh Cavalry under George Armstrong Custer. In the days to come, his own Lakota people and all the world would know that name as it was said in English: Crazy Horse.

Star Boy
Cheyenne

Two young women walked out on the prairie one
night to look up at the stars.

"I like that red star there," one of the young women
said.

"I like that bright star better," said the other. "I wish
it would come down to earth and marry me."

The next day, when they were gathering buffalo chips
for the cooking fires, they saw a porcupine in the top of
a small aspen tree.

"Let us try to shake it down to get some of its quills
for decoration," the first young woman said.

"No," the second young woman said, "I will climb up
and knock it off the limb with a stick." Then she began
to climb. But the higher she climbed, the farther away
the porcupine seemed to be. She looked down and saw
that the tree was growing, carrying her far up into the
sky. It took her right through the clouds, into the sky
land. The young woman glanced around. The land was
very much like the earth. The porcupine was no longer
anywhere to be seen, but as she looked, she noticed
someone walking toward her. It was an older man
dressed in white skins. He took her by the hand.

"I heard you say you wished to marry me," he said.
"Now you will be my wife. You will remain here in the
sky land with me for the rest of your life."

For a while, the young woman lived happily with
White Star. Her own name was now Star Woman, and
the other people in the sky land treated her with respect
because she was the wife of their chief. Although her
husband was much older, he was always kind to her.
After a year had passed, she gave birth to a baby boy. He

was a strong and happy child like any other baby boy, except for one thing. On his forehead was a birthmark shaped like a star. Because he was the son of White Star, the sky chief, he was given the birthmark to show that he would have great power when he came of age. Star Woman was delighted with her child, but she began to think sadly of her own mother. My mother will never see her own grandson, she thought. Star Woman began to grow homesick for her people and wished she could return to them.

"I am going to dig roots," she said to White Star.

"That is good," he answered. "But do not try to dig up that plant with the red at its base. Its root is so deep that if it is dug out, it will make a hole in the sky."

Star Woman took her digging stick and went out looking for roots. As soon as she saw the plant with red at its base, she began to dig it up. It was not easy, but finally she was able to pull it out.

Where the plant had been, there was now a hole in the sky land. Far below she could see a circle of many lodges, and she knew it was the camp of her own people. She put the plant back into its hole and went to the lodge of White Star. There she began to make a rope by weaving together the grasses that grew in the sky land. Every day her rope was longer.

Finally she could wait no more. She was sure her rope was long enough. She took her baby and returned to that plant with the red at its base. She pulled it out and lowered her rope. It seemed as if it touched the earth below. She tied the end to a stick that she placed across the hole, and began to lower her baby and herself down.

When she got to the bottom, she was still high above the ground. Star Woman was not strong enough to climb back up. She held on for a time and then fell. It was a long fall. Star Woman was killed, but her baby survived.

The meadowlarks found the child and took pity on him. They fed him and kept him warm. As he grew stronger, he followed the birds as they flew, running beneath them. At last it came time for the birds to fly to the south land.

"I will come with you," said the boy.

"No," the meadowlarks said. "You've become tall and strong, but you are not a bird. Now you must return to your own people. You will learn how to become a man among them. Follow the river downstream and you will come to their camp circle."

Then the meadowlarks gave the boy a gift. They used some of their own feathers to make arrows and gave him a small, strong bow. "Use these to help your people and do not forget us," they told him.

The meadowlarks flew south, leaving Star Boy behind. Ever since then, the people have known that it is wrong to kill meadowlarks. And if you listen to their calls closely, you will hear that those birds know how to speak Cheyenne.

Star Boy began to follow the creek downstream. He walked a long way until he came to the edge of a big camp. There was a small teepee, and the door flap was open, so the boy walked in. An old woman was seated by the fire. She gestured for the boy to sit in the place of honor.

"Grandmother," Star Boy said, "I have come far to find you."

"Grandson," the old woman said, "I am glad you have come here. I would offer you water to drink, but there is a great sucking monster that lives in the river. Whenever people go to get water, it sucks them in. Now all of the people in the village have been swallowed, and I am about to die of thirst."

"Grandmother," the boy said, "give me your bucket. I will go and bring water back to you."

Star Boy walked down to the stream. He bent over and began to dip the bucket into the water. As soon as he did so, the sucking monster opened its big mouth and drew him in. But Star Boy had brought his fire-making kit and tinder with him. He made a fire, and by its light he saw that all the people the monster had swallowed were there in its belly with him.

Star Boy looked around until he saw a place in the sucking monster's side that looked weak. He took out his stone knife and cut a hole. As soon as he did this, the monster floated up to the surface of the river and died. Star Boy walked out of the sucking monster, and all the people who had been inside followed him. He bent down and filled his bucket, and then returned to the camp with the rest of his people.

"Grandmother," he said, "here is your water to drink. The sucking monster will bother the people no longer."

"Grandson," said the old woman, "you have done well. It would be good to make a great fire and dance about it to celebrate your brave deed. But we cannot get more wood for a fire because of Great Owl. Great Owl lives in the timber. Whenever people try to go into the woods, it swoops down and carries them to its nest, where it eats them."

"I will go and get wood," Star Boy said. He hung his bow and arrows over his shoulder and went out into the forest, where he began to chop wood. Before long, the

Great Owl heard the sound of Star Boy's stone ax. It floated down on silent wings, grabbed him in its talons, and began to fly to its nest. But Star Boy fitted an arrow to the string of his bow and shot it. The Great Owl fell to the earth, dead.

When Star Boy came back to the camp circle, he was carrying a great load of firewood.

"Grandmother," he said, "I have killed the Great Owl. No longer will it keep the people from getting firewood."

Then a great fire was built, and the camp crier went about calling everyone to rejoice. All the people came together and praised Star Boy. They danced and laughed and told stories until the sun rose the next day.

But when the sun rose, Star Boy was hungry.

"Grandmother," he said, "I am in need of food. Is there no buffalo meat?"

"Grandson," the old woman said, "there is no food in this camp. Whenever the men go out to hunt buffalo, the White Crow flies down and chases the animals far away. So we have no food to eat."

"Grandmother," said Star Boy, "let me take that old buffalo robe. I will see what I can do about the White Crow."

Then Star Boy put the buffalo robe over his shoulders and crept near the buffalo. He mingled in with the herd, and none of the buffalo paid any special attention to the old buffalo with the dirty hair that had just joined them. Before long, though, some young men came out from the Cheyenne village to hunt the buffalo. Before they could get close enough, a big white bird flew down to the buffalo herd.

"Run, run," White Crow cawed. "Run, run."

The buffalo herd began to run, and the old buffalo with the dirty hair ran with them. They left the Cheyenne hunters, who could not run as fast, far behind. But soon the old buffalo began to lag behind. Then it stumbled and fell.

White Crow flew down and began to circle over the old buffalo. "Are you dead, dead, dead?" White Crow cawed. "Are you dead, dead, dead?" The old buffalo did not move. Four times White Crow circled and called, but the buffalo did not move. At last White Crow settled down and landed on the old buffalo's back. He hopped up toward its head. As soon as he did so, Star Boy reached up from beneath the buffalo robe and grabbed White Crow by the legs. He tied White Crow's wings and carried him back to the camp.

"Here is your enemy," Star Boy said, and he handed White Crow over to the head of the Dog Soldiers, the society of men whose job it was to protect the people.

"I'll hang him over the smoke hole in my lodge until we decide what to do with him," the head of the Dog Soldiers said. Then he carried White Crow to his lodge and tied him up where the smoke was rising out of the lodge. White Crow hung there upside down, the smoke blackening his feathers. It was so hot in the smoke hole that White Crow grew smaller. The cords around him loosened and he became free. But he was White Crow no longer. Now he was black, as all crows are to this day. And he was no longer able to drive away the buffalo as he had when his feathers were white.

Once again the people could go out and hunt the buffalo with success. They were able to bring down enough buffalo to provide food for everyone in the village. As the people feasted, however, Star Boy's grandmother did not look happy.

"Grandmother," Star Boy asked, "what is wrong?"

"It is Winter Man," she said. "He is going to come soon. The snow will grow deep, and we will not be able to hunt the buffalo. Then he will begin to kill our people, especially the old ones such as me."

"Grandmother," Star Boy said, "come hunting with me. I will see what I can do about Winter Man."

Star Boy and his grandmother went out together to follow the buffalo. When they were far from the camp circle, Star Boy was able to kill a fat cow.

"Now we will cut this one up, Grandmother," he said. Yet as soon as the old woman began to butcher the buffalo cow, Winter Man walked over the hill. He was a giant taller than any man. He had a great club in his hand, and the north wind was at his back.

When he saw the old woman, he shouted, "Old woman, I am going to take that fat buffalo."

Star Boy's grandmother stood as if to run away, but Star Boy stopped her.

"I will stand by you, Grandmother," he said.

Winter Man came and stood over them. "This old woman has been walking around too long," he said. Winter Man lifted his club to strike, but Star Boy looked at him and his arm fell off. He lifted his other arm, and it dropped off, too. He tried to shout, and his head fell to the ground. Then, riding on the wind, Winter Man's wife came, grabbed the pieces of her husband, and carried him back over the hill.

Star Boy and his grandmother finished butchering the cow, wrapped the meat in its hide, made a travois, and dragged it back to camp. When they had shared the meat

with the people, Star Boy turned again to his grandmother.

"Grandmother," he asked, "where does Winter Man
live?"

"You must not go there," said the old woman. "He
will have his great bow, and he will kill you because of
what you did to him."

"Grandmother," Star Boy asked again, "where does
Winter Man live?"

"You must not go there," the old woman repeated. "If
Winter Man does not kill you, then his wife will kill
you. She is as bad as her husband."

"Grandmother," Star Boy asked a third time, "where
does Winter Man live?"

"You must not go there," the old woman said yet
again. "All of his children are there and they are also
dangerous."

The fourth time Star Boy asked the question, his
grandmother finally told him.

"He lives in that cave alongside the river," she said.

Then Star Boy went straight to that cave. He walked
inside, where Winter Man was being healed by his
wife's medicine.

"Why are you here?" Winter Man roared, reaching for
his great bow.

But Star Boy was faster than Winter Man. He grabbed
the great bow before the giant was able to reach it.

"Uncle," Star Boy said, lifting up the bow, which was
as big as a lodgepole pine log, "why is your bow so
weak?" And he broke Winter Man's bow as easily as if
it were a twig.

"Why are you in my lodge?" Winter Man roared
again, reaching for his club.

Once more Star Boy was too quick. He grabbed the

club and raised it. "I have come to see how you are feeling, Uncle," he said. Then he struck Winter Man and killed him. He turned and struck Winter Man's wife, who was about to hit him with her own club. He killed almost all of Winter Man's children as they tried to kill him. And if he had killed all of those Winter Giants, winter would never again have come to the lands of the Cheyenne. But one small Winter Giant slipped out through a crack in the back of the cave. To this day he returns every year, and though he is not as fierce as his father, he is still dangerous, especially to the old people.

Then Star Boy returned to the village. Everyone celebrated his great victory. When several moons had passed, however, Star Boy looked up into the sky and knew that he could stay no longer. He went one last time to his grandmother's teepee.

"Grandmother," Star Boy said, "I have done all I can do among my mother's relatives. I have become a man here among the people of the Striped Arrows, but now I must go back to the land of my father."

With that, he began heading toward the east. He walked and walked until he was out of sight. And it is said that he traveled until he walked back up into the sky land. There, like his father, he became a star. Today he is the North Star and he can be seen every night, looking down from the center of the sky land on the camp circles of the Cheyenne.

Salmon Boy
Tlingit

One day, in the village of Sitka, a boy asked his mother for some food. It had been a long time since the salmon run, so all that she had was some dry salmon, which she gave to the boy.

"This is half-moldy," the boy said. "I will not eat half-moldy fish." He threw it on the ground and then stepped on it.

"The salmon *qwani* do not like to be treated that way," the mother said. "Whatever salmon we have to eat, we must be thankful for. We do not throw food away. If we throw food away, bad things may happen."

The boy, who was close to the time when he would be a young man, ignored her. He walked down to the water to try to catch some sea gulls with fish eggs on a small hook. He wrapped his line tightly around his wrist, baited his hook, and threw it into the water near the gulls.

Suddenly a huge sea gull, bigger than any bird he had ever seen before, grabbed his line and pulled him into the water before he could cut himself free. He tried to swim to shore, but the current was strong and the cold water deep. He called for help, but none of the people was near the water and no one heard him.

As he sank, a canoe full of strange-looking people came to him under the water. They were wearing clothing that shone as brightly as the scales of fish in the sun. It was the salmon *qwani*, the souls of the salmon that had died after swimming upstream to spawn. They pulled him into their canoe.

"Half-Moldy Boy," they said, laughing, "come with us."

Then the salmon people carried him out into the ocean to their village. The souls of the salmon looked just like people to the boy. Their village was much like his own village of Sitka. Although they called him Half-Moldy Boy, the salmon people treated him well.

"You must stay here with us now," they said. Then they showed him to a small house where he could stay. After a time, the boy became hungry. There was no food in the house. He looked all around the village.

"I am hungry. What can I eat?" Half-Moldy Boy finally said to one of the salmon people.

"You see those people there?" the salmon person said to him. "Just go over and say you want to wrestle with them. After a while, because you are strong, you will get a good hold and throw your opponent down. He will become food, which you may eat. Carry it away from the village and make a fire to cook it. But remember to burn all of the bones in that fire when you are through. Then come right back to our village and you will be surprised at what you see."

Half-Moldy Boy did as he was told. He wrestled with one of the young salmon men. When he threw that young man down, his opponent seemed to disappear. All that was left was a salmon at his feet. He carried it away, cooked it, and ate it. When he was done, Half-Moldy Boy was so eager to return to the village and see whatever it was that would surprise him that he hurriedly gathered the bones together and threw them quickly into the fire. When he arrived at the village, the young salmon man he had thrown down had already returned. But he was bent over, holding his back.

"Ah," the man said, "my backbone is hurting me."

Then Half-Moldy Boy realized he had been in such a hurry that he had not been careful enough. He quickly ran back to where he had eaten the salmon. There he discovered one tiny bone he had missed and threw it into the fire. When he returned again to the village, he found that the man's backache had disappeared.

As the days passed, Half-Moldy Boy was taught many things by the salmon people. He learned that there were songs and prayers of thanksgiving that a good fisherman must know. He tried to memorize them all so he would be able to take them back to his people. With those prayers and songs, his people would be able to do much better when they went fishing for salmon.

One day, many of the salmon people in the village started getting into their canoes.

"Where are you going?" Half-Moldy Boy asked.

"We are going to Copper River," one group said.

"We are going up to Dry Bay," said another.

So the salmon people spoke, referring to each stream where there would be a salmon run. Finally one group said, "We are going to the little river by Sitka."

"I will come with you," said Half-Moldy Boy. He climbed into a canoe and paddled with the others. All around him were many canoes filled with salmon returning home from the sea. The groups were going to the rivers where they had been born.

As the group he was with approached their river, the salmon people spoke with excitement about the coming battle.

"There will be forts in the river to stop us," they said, and the boy realized they were speaking about fish traps.

Every now and then, one of the salmon would tell another, "Ehaw! Stand up in the canoe and look around." And the boy would realize that meant jumping up out of the stream.

Soon they were in the river by Sitka. The boy saw his own mother there on the bank. He quickly stood up in the canoe, and his mother caught him as he leaped from the river.

"Look at the fine fish I have caught," she shouted to her husband. Then her husband noticed the copper necklace on the fish.

"What does this mean?" he asked, pointing to the necklace. "This is the necklace our son wore."

"Ehaw!" Salmon Boy's mother cried. "This is my son."

The two of them carried Salmon Boy home. They placed him on a shelf inside their house, surrounding him with eagle feathers. Then they called for the shaman. When the old man came in, he went straight to the shelf and examined Salmon Boy.

"It is my son," said the mother.

"I see who he is," the shaman said. "If you do as I say, he will be well." He heated oil in the fire and placed four drops on Salmon Boy as he lay there. With each drop, Salmon Boy grew a little larger. At last, the old shaman stepped back. "Cover him and leave him for the night," the old man said.

All through the night, the parents waited for dawn, praying that their son would be well. Every now and then, a noise would come from the shelf where Salmon Boy lay, but the parents did not uncover him.

When the dawn came, the parents removed the cover.

There was their son, fully human again. They lifted him up, and he embraced them.

"I have come back to help our people," Salmon Boy said.

From that day on, Salmon Boy always remembered the care one must take never to waste food and never, never to offend the souls of the salmon.

Tommy's Whale
Inupiaq

Tommy Anawrok had never gone out to hunt the bowhead before. But now he was about to climb into the umiak, the walrus-skin boat, with his uncle and his uncle's crew. His uncle had hunted whales for many years and was one of the most respected captains. Today they would go out into the Open Lead, where the ice had thawed and the whales would come to the surface.

Although Tommy was only thirteen and had never before gone on a whale hunt, he had known the bowhead whale all of his life. When he was six years old, a whale was brought up on the ice by his father's crew, and his father had taken the boy aside.

"My son," he said, "I want you to know the whale. We are going to leave this whale on the ice until you have touched every part of its body."

Tommy did as his father said. He spent a long time with the great whale there in the almost endless Arctic day of late May. He touched its flukes and its tail. He felt its mouth and the baleen through which it strained its food. He climbed onto the whale's back and walked up it, and found the place just where the head joined the body, where there was a small indentation. His father had told him to look for that place. In the old days, when a whale was struck badly and was suffering, the bravest and the best of the whalers would jump onto the whale's back and drive his harpoon down into that place. Then the whale's pain would be ended and it would die.

When he finished, the long day's light was dim and his father took him home and told him to sleep. That

night he dreamed that he was a whale swimming
beneath the ice, waiting to be called up by the people
when they needed his help.

Tommy looked at the broad back of his uncle Tinuk,
who sat in the front of the umiak. Tommy had great
respect for his uncle. He found himself remembering
words Uncle Tinuk had said to him long ago. "The
greatest of all the sea animals is the bowhead whale.
Long ago, when the Great Spirit had made all things, the
Creator decided to make one more being, more beautiful
and perfect than all the others. That being was the bowhead whale. Then the Creator saw that the Inupiaq
people needed to hunt the whale to survive, and so the
Creator gave them permission. But it was with the
understanding that we would always show the whale
respect.

"The Europeans have tried to separate us from the
animals, from the sea," Uncle Tinuk had continued,
"but every time they take an Inupiaq away from that
life, they take a part of his spirit. Those animals are our
lives in every way. We hunt them only because we need
them to survive. That is why we use every part of an
animal after we kill it, and we show it respect and
thank its spirit."

Tommy had listened closely. He was only seven then,
but he already knew that he would be a good hunter
someday if he could be like his uncle. His mother had
once told him a story about Uncle Tinuk.

"When your Uncle Tinuk was a boy," she had said,
"he would go out hunting for seals with his gun. One
time he went out with two of his older friends. Tinuk
waited near one of the breathing holes for a seal to come

out so that he could shoot it. His friends went around one of the pressure ridges on the ice, where the ice was pushed up twice as high as the roof of our house, to look for other breathing holes there. When they climbed up on top of the pressure ridge, they saw a polar bear only about fifty yards from Tinuk. It was down on its belly, crawling toward Tinuk the way a bear will when it is sneaking up on a seal. It was too far off for the other boys to shoot at it, and the wind was strong in their faces, so that they knew Tinuk would not hear their shouts. They could only watch.

"It seemed as if Tinuk did not see that bear. He kept sitting there, looking at the breathing hole in the ice. He did not move, and the bear got closer. Then, just when the bear was close enough to charge, Tinuk fired that little twenty-two. It hit the bear in its eye and killed it, like that. Tinuk had been waiting for the right time to shoot."

"It is true," Tommy's grandmother Belle had said from where she sat near the stove, sewing on a reindeer skin. "That is what my son did. He was like that boy in the story with the great eagle. He did not strike too soon."

Tommy knew that story about the great eagle. Grandma Belle told it often and Tommy never tired of it. Long ago, the whales began to vanish from the sea. The Inupiaq people lived near the foot of the big mountains by the sea. On top of one mountain a giant eagle lived, and down that mountainside a river ran. But instead of water, that river was full of whale oil. When the people saw oil in the river, they knew that the great eagle was catching all the whales and carrying them to the mountaintop.

The people knew that soon all the whales would be gone. So it was decided that someone must kill the great eagle. A boy whose name was Tinuk—the same name as Tommy's uncle—was the one who said he would go.

Tinuk took two spears and climbed the mountain and waited in a crevice. When the great eagle returned, carrying two whales in its talons, Tinuk did not move. Finally the eagle settled down. At just the right moment, Tinuk struck with his first spear. It wounded the eagle, which screamed and spread its wings to take flight. Then Tinuk stood so the angry eagle could see him. He waited as the eagle swooped toward him. Then he threw his spear, piercing its breast and killing it.

As Tommy joined the men in the umiak, he found himself remembering the story of the eagle. The importance of trusting himself was part of what it had taught him. But even more, the story had taught him that one could trust oneself only when prepared. The life of a hunter was dangerous. Anything might happen at any moment. Knowing what his body could do, knowing that his weapons were in good working order, knowing about the animals and the ice, the wind and the sea, were all necessary if he hoped to feed his family and return home safely. When a man went out in a small boat, he went only with men he knew would not foolishly put themselves or the others with them into a dangerous situation. That was the trust his uncle was showing him today.

The clouds hung low in the gray sky. The water of the Open Lead, the river of seawater that flowed through the ice at this time of year, was calm. The men's snowmobiles with their sleds attached to the back, burdened with ropes and the block and tackle to pull a whale up on the ice, shrank until they could no longer be seen.

"Keep watching to all sides," Uncle Tinuk said, and Tommy narrowed his eyes behind the dark lenses. Like his uncle, he wore sunglasses against the glare. In the old days, the Inupiaq had made their own "sunglasses," carved with a small slit in the center, which were strapped over the eyes. Two of the old men still had such goggles. But most of the best hunters now used modern sunglasses. He lifted his head up even higher to keep watch.

Fred Anawrok, his older cousin, chuckled from behind him. "Tommy," he said, his left hand steady on the handle of the outboard motor, "you look like that big eagle your grandma tells about in that story."

"There." Tommy's uncle spoke from the front of the umiak. The motor roared, and they turned hard to the starboard side. There were two whales ahead of them, swimming on the surface. As they came closer, Uncle Tinuk raised the gun to his shoulder, aiming for the spot that would kill the whale as quickly as possible. It was not right that any animal should suffer, even though it was necessary to hunt it.

Tommy held his breath, waiting for the shot. But his uncle kept waiting. Then, as the whale surged up, he fired. The blast of his shot rang in Tommy's ears. Just as he fired, however, the boat struck a wave and drifted away from the whale. They brought the boat close again. A second shot was fired. It, too, went wrong. The whale continued to swim, its blood flowing into the sea.

The long harpoons in the boat could be used now, but the strike would have to be clean and sure to kill the whale. Suddenly Tommy knew what he had to do. He stood and called to his uncle.

"Give me the harpoon," he said.

Uncle Tinuk and the others in the umiak looked at him. Everything was silent. It seemed as if even the sound of the outboard motor and the splashing of the whale as it swam were gone.

Uncle Tinuk took the harpoon and thrust it, point first, at Tommy. It was a gesture that might have made another person sit back down or flinch, but Tommy reached out his hand for the harpoon. He took the cold metal in his hand, and a look passed between him and his uncle. Uncle Tinuk understood that now was Tommy's time to try. Holding the harpoon across his body for balance, Tommy moved toward the starboard side of the umiak where the whale swam. He took a deep breath and jumped. All of the balance that hunters train for served him well. He landed on the whale's back and did not fall off, even though the water washed over his ankles and his knees. He made his way up the whale's back until he stood over the place he had touched when he was a small boy, that indentation where the whale's head joined its body. He lifted the harpoon.

Then, with all of his might, he struck down. The sharp harpoon plunged through the skin and fat and bone. The whale quivered once, the full length of its huge body, and then died.

Tommy felt hands grasping him, pulling him into the umiak. His uncle and his cousin were patting him on the back as the other men fastened the ropes to the bowhead to tow it onto the ice. But Tommy saw only the great whale, and he spoke the words he had learned long ago.

"Bowhead," he said, "thank you for giving us our lives."

AFTERWORD

I owe much to the elders who shared stories with me, but I could not have told the ones in this collection had it not been for my two sons, who helped me better realize what I had been taught as I tried to pass it on to them.

I listened to many voices as I put this book together. Some were the voices of teachers who had, in a physical sense, passed on. But I only needed to be silent for a moment to hear again the gentle and strong voice of my friend Swift Eagle, the Apache/Pueblo storyteller who once reminded me to listen to the voice of the leaves. In that same silence, I could also hear the clear, teaching words of Maurice Dennis, the Abenaki tradition-bearer whose Indian name, Mdawelasis, means "Little Loon." And there were others, so many I cannot list them all.

I tried, as I wrote, to keep in mind the meaning of the name given to me a decade ago by Clan Mother Dewasentah of the Onondaga Nation. That name, Gah-neh-goh-he-yoh, means "The Good Mind." To keep a good mind means that one must always try to speak with honesty and honor and keep one's thoughts away from selfishness and vanity, especially when speaking on a topic as important as the passage of a boy from childhood into young manhood.

With that in mind, it is important for me to say one more thing. All of these stories are wiser than I am. Their messages come from many generations, and if these tellings of mine have meaning for those who read them, it is only because I have succeeded to some small extent in being true to the original voices that spoke them.

There is such a wealth of traditions and so many hundreds of volumes devoted to the stories of different Native American nations that a truly representative bibliography would be far too long to include. Further, many books put together by non-Natives during the nineteenth and twentieth centuries have mistold Native stories. I strongly urge readers to turn to books written by Native people themselves. There is a new generation of Native American writers and storytellers whose work is both accurate and exciting. An excellent introduction to many of the central ideas of Native American life, including material on storytelling and rites of passage, is *The Sacred* by Peggy Beck, Anna Lee Walters, and Nia Francisco (Tsaile, Ariz.: Navajo Community College Press, 1977).

Some other books of interest are:

Erdoes, Richard, and Alfonso Ortiz, eds. *American Indian Myths and Legends*, New York: Pantheon Books, 1984.

Hilbert, Vi, trans. and ed. *Haboo: Native American Stories from Puget Sound*, Seattle: University of Washington Press, 1985.

Tehanetorens. *Tales of the Iroquois*, Rooseveltown, N.Y: Akwesasne Notes Press, 1976.

Zuni People. *The Zunis: Self-Portrayals*, Albuquerque: University of New Mexico Press, 1972.

About the Author

Joseph Bruchac is a storyteller and writer whose work often draws upon his Native American heritage. His stories and poems have appeared in more than four hundred anthologies, and he has written several books, including *Thirteen Moons on Turtle's Back* and the *Keepers of the Earth* series, coauthored with Michael Caduto. Mr. Bruchac is the recipient of the American Book Award for editing *Breaking Silence*, an anthology of Asian-American poetry; the Parents' Choice Award for *Gluskabe Stories*, a storytelling tape of traditional Abenaki tales; and the Hope S. Dean Memorial Award from the Foundation for Children's Books for developing a body of work that promotes an appreciation of children's literature. Mr. Bruchac lives in Greenfield, New York, with his wife, Carol, and their two sons, Jesse and Jim.